The Logic of Chinese Characters Mnemonic Method for Learning Chinese Characters

"No part of this book may be scanned, reproduced, or distributed in any printed or electronic form without the prior permission of the author."

Copyright © 2023 Jonathan Contreras Espinoza
All rights reserved. Stamp: Independently published
Sello: Independently published

Private Chinese Classes
WhatsApp

Books to Learn Chinese
Amazon

Videos to Learn Chinese
Youtube

Discovering China
instagram

TABLE OF CONTENTS

一 Prologue 1
- 1.1 A record of ideas
- 1.2 Evolution of Chinese characters

二 Introducción 4
- 2.1 Classify characters by frequency of use
- 2.2 Pictographic characters
- 2.3 Associative characters
- 2.4 Teaching new vocabulary
- 2.5 Use of simple language and visual support

三 Introduction to the study of Chinese characters 6
- 3.1 Pictographic or Ideographic characters
- 3.2 Indicative characters
- 3.3 Associative characters
- 3.4 Picto-phonetic characters
- 3.5 Characters with extended meaning
- 3.6 Borrowed characters

四 How to use this book 8

五 Main content 10

六 Alphabetical index 118

PROLOGUE

The little boy sitting at the desk is the living embodiment of mental concentration. He rests his left hand on a sheet of large-gridded rice paper. His head is tilted slightly to the left, and his eyes are focused on the tip of a brush made from a thin bamboo stalk, which he holds vertically in his right hand. He moves the brush slowly and deliberately, dipping it into an inkwell at intervals. With great care, he is endeavoring to learn to write... in Chinese.

To the Western eye, whatever may be written on the paper might seem complicated to the point of being impossible to understand and utterly confusing. Nevertheless, through relentless practice and repetition, the young boy, like millions of other Chinese students, is learning, perhaps in the only practical way, the rudiments of Chinese writing.

A Record of Ideas

What sets the Chinese language apart from most other languages is the fact that it lacks an alphabet. Because of this, Chinese characters are not written by simply spelling out sounds, as is done in Spanish or other languages with alphabets. Essentially, Chinese writing is not a record of spoken sounds but rather a record of ideas.

In the language of linguists, Chinese writing is ideographic, or writing of ideas. Each word or character, through its form and appearance, conveys a certain idea to the reader. If the idea is simple, the character representing it might simply be a pictorial representation.

Linguists refer to this type of characters as pictographic, or writing through drawings. Among such characters are words that refer to common objects known in daily life, such as: 日 (Sun), 月 (Moon), 木 (Tree), 人 (Person), 口 (Mouth).

When looking at the words presented above, you may recognize them as drawings, or perhaps not. This is because, over the years, these pictographic words have undergone successive stages in which they have been simplified to make them easier to write. But if you were to examine the oldest versions of these words, it would become quite evident that they are indeed drawings. In the table that will appear on the next page, you will see the changes through which some characters have passed, from purely pictorial characters, which are shown on the left side of the table, to acquiring the stylized form used today.

Obviously, a writing system composed solely of words consisting of drawings would be very limited since there are only a certain number of ideas that can be represented by simple drawings. Therefore, to express more complicated and abstract ideas, characters usually consist of several simple pictographic words arranged in such a way that people can recognize the ideas, based on their own common experience. For example, the "Sun" (日) and the "Moon" (月) together mean "bright" (明), the "man" (人) leaning against a "tree" (木) means "rest" (休).

It may be easy to understand why these two characters are formed this way. In times past, when life was simpler, there was probably nothing brighter than the Sun or the Moon, and a brief pause under a tree provided rest.

EVOLUTION OF CHINESE CHARACTERS

☀ → ⊙ → ⊙ → 日 → 日 ⟶ 日 (Rì) Sun

👁 → ⌔ → ⌔ → 目 → 目 ⟶ 目 (Mù) Eye

🌳 → 朩 → 木 → 木 → 木 ⟶ 木 (Mù) Tree

⛰ → ▲ → 山 → 山 → 山 ⟶ 山 (Shān) Mountain

🐎 → 馬 → 馬 → 馬 → 馬 ⟶ 马 (Mǎ) Horse

🗡 → 丿 → 丿 → 刀 → 刀 ⟶ 力 (Lì) Force, power

🐟 → 魚 → 魚 → 魚 → 魚 ⟶ 鱼 (Yú) Fish

🚪 → 門 → 門 → 門 → 門 ⟶ 门 (Mén) Door

INTRODUCTION

"The Logic of Chinese Characters - Mnemonic Method for Learning" is a manual designed to facilitate the memorization and understanding of Chinese characters. This innovative method employs various pedagogical techniques that make learning to read Chinese characters accessible to anyone. Below are some of the techniques used:

- **Classify characters by frequency of use**: The book begins by teaching the most common and widely used characters, so that students can quickly identify the largest number of characters in various texts and contexts, such as newspapers, books, the internet, etc.

- **Pictographic characters**: Priority is given to teaching characters that graphically represent objects, such as 口 (Kǒu) which means "mouth", 人 (Rén) which means "man", 日 (Rì) which means "sun", and 火 (Huǒ) which means "fire". These characters are easier to recognize and remember due to their visual nature.

- **Associative characters**: The formation of characters through the combination of two or more ideographic characters is explored. This approach uses historical data and imagination to make learning more interesting and natural. For example, the character 明 (Míng), meaning "bright", is formed by combining 日 (Rì) representing the "sun" and 月 (Yuè) representing the "moon", the two brightest celestial bodies in the sky.

Another example is 鸣 (Míng), which means "the voice or cry of a bird", formed by the combination of 口 (Kǒu) meaning "mouth" and 鸟 (Niǎo) meaning "bird".

- **Teaching of new vocabulary**: derived from the combination of learned characters, with an explanation of the logic behind the union of these disyllabic words, formed by two or even more characters. For example, let's consider the character 毛 (Máo), which means hair, and the character 笔 (Bǐ), which means writing instrument. From their combination arises the word 毛笔. Another illustrative case is the word 手机 (Shǒujī), which translates to mobile phone. This word results from the union of 手 (Shǒu), meaning hand, and 机 (jī), meaning machine. Therefore, the literal translation would be "machine of the hand", which makes a lot of sense, especially nowadays, as we always carry the mobile phone in our hand.

- **Use of simple language and visual support**: The book employs clear explanations and simple language to ensure understanding. Additionally, illustrations are used to encourage the retention of characters, making learning more visual and appealing.

In summary, "The Logic of Chinese Characters" offers a comprehensive and user-friendly approach to learning the Chinese language's writing system, providing students with the necessary tools to remember and understand characters effectively.

Introduction to the Study of Chinese Characters

Chinese characters are the oldest writing system still in use, as they have been continuously utilized, with variations, since around 1200 BCE to the present day. Chinese writing is based on a system of pictograms and ideograms created 3,200 years ago, which evolved in form and function over the centuries to meet the cultural and communicative needs of the Chinese people.

A Chinese character is basically a pictogram in its written form, a syllable or phonetic unit in its spoken form, and a specific meaning or concept in its semantic part. The evolution of language led to most words containing two characters, and thus being disyllabic; it also caused a continuous simplification of primitive pictograms, rendering them unrecognizable to the untrained eye.

Traditionally, Chinese characters have been divided into six types based on their origin:

1. Pictographic or Ideographic Characters: These are pictograms whose form is related to the object they represent. They are the oldest and easiest characters to recognize.

2. Indicative Characters: These are characters formed by an ideogram that suggests their meaning.

3. Associative Characters: These are characters in which two or more simple characters are combined to create a new character, whose meaning is related to those that formed it.

4. Picto-phonetic Characters: These are created with one phonetic element and another semantic one.

5. Characters with extended meaning: These are those in which their extended sense is emphasized to include similar concepts.

6. Borrowed Characters: Borrowed, for various reasons, usually due to identical pronunciation, but with a meaning different from what they originally had.

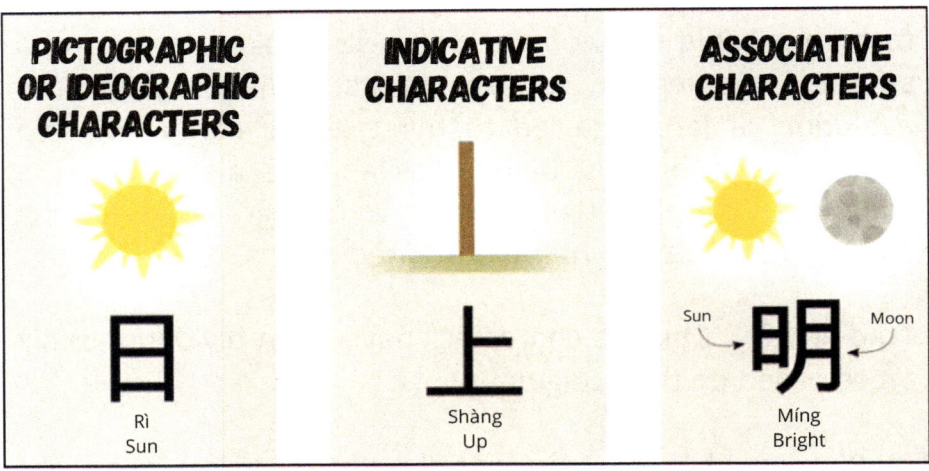

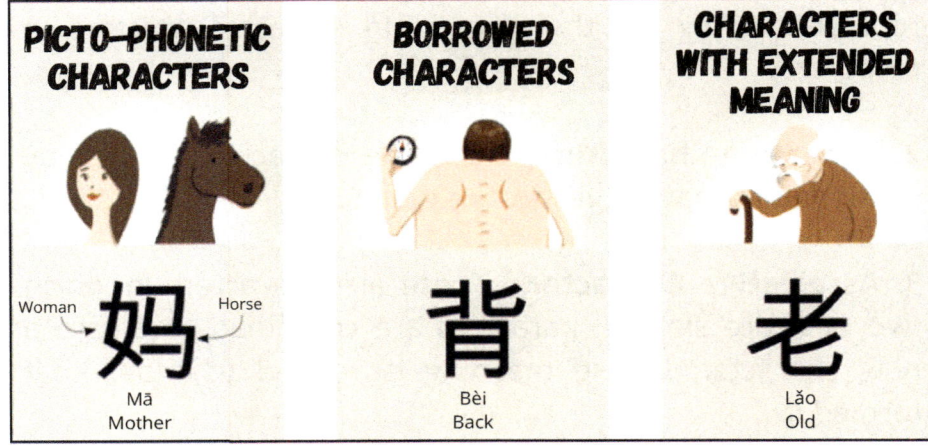

This book does not solely focus on the evolution of Chinese characters or the various changes and reforms that Chinese writing has undergone throughout its extensive history. Instead, it aims to provide a method of rapid, simple, and direct teaching, with the goal of empowering the reader to master the art of reading Chinese characters, so that they can use it as a valuable tool not only in the workplace and academia but also in any field that requires the ability to understand and read Chinese writing.

With the intention of achieving this noble purpose, I have taken the liberty of employing explanations that are both plausible and widely circulated among scholars regarding the origin of characters. This approach aims to facilitate the retention of both pronunciation and meaning of each character. However, beyond these conventional explanations, I have decided to incorporate a fundamental element that has been inherent to the essence of Chinese characters for millennia: interpretation and imagination. Always aiming to facilitate retention and memorization. I hope this book proves useful on your journey to understanding the logic of Chinese characters.

Jonathan Contreras

HOW TO USE THIS BOOK

This manual is a tool that, while it can be used as a dictionary to randomly look up Chinese characters, reaches its maximum utility when studying each character in the established order of presentation. At this point, it is important to understand that the only effective way to learn Chinese characters, both for reading and writing, is by approaching them individually, one by one. This method of learning is common among both Chinese language learners and native Chinese speakers when learning characters in primary school.

The design of this manual is geared towards initially introducing the most common and widely used characters, gradually advancing to the more complex and specific ones. This order has been structured with the purpose of making the learning of the Chinese language more accessible, especially in the beginning, when it may seem challenging.

The importance of following the established order in the book lies in the fact that, when associative characters that form a new character are presented, these elements will have already been introduced individually beforehand. This facilitates the understanding of these new characters, significantly contributing to the learning process.

Another aspect to consider when following the book's established order for learning characters is that the examples of words for the new characters only employ characters that have already been taught and learned.

In this way, the example words are not only useful for understanding the new character itself, but also for reviewing the characters previously learned.

For practicing the writing of Chinese characters, we recommend using a grid notebook with guidelines known in Chinese as 田字格 (Tiánzìgé). The series of notebooks "Chinese Character Calligraphy Notebook Tiánzìgé 田字格 Common Chinese Characters: Hànzì 汉字" follows the same method as this manual and presents the characters from the most common and used to the more complex and specific, with the aim of facilitating their study. This series of notebooks is divided into five parts:

1. Chinese Character Writing Workbook.Most Common Chinese Characters Hànzì 汉字 1 to 100
   (ISBN: B0CRJG2KDZ)

2. Chinese Character Writing Workbook.Most Common Chinese Characters Hànzì 汉字 101 to 200
   (ISBN: B0CRJ4GHCM)

3. Chinese Character Writing Workbook.Most Common Chinese Characters Hànzì 汉字 201 to 300
   (ISBN: B0CRJ4H7S9)

4. Chinese Character Writing Workbook.Most Common Chinese Characters Hànzì 汉字 301 to 400
   (ISBN: B0CRLXCC6L)

5. Chinese Character Writing Workbook.Most Common Chinese Characters Hànzì 汉字 401 to 500
   (ISBN: B0CRKHLCQG)

The Logic of Chinese Characters

1. 人 (Rén) Person, human being.

Note: Pictogram of a standing **person**. When it is part of another character, its writing is simplified as 亻.

2. 口 (Kǒu) Mouth, exit, entry, measurement word for family members.

Note: Pictogram of an open **mouth**. Its extended meaning is any type of entry.

3. 日 (Rì) Day, sun.

Note: Pictogram of the **sun** with a ray of light in the center.

4. 土 (Tǔ) Soil, earth, Land, territory.

Note: Pictogram of a mound of earth, which was used in ancient times to mark the **territory** belonging to someone in particular.

The Logic of Chinese Characters

5. 大 (Dà) Big, large.

Note: Pictogram of a person (人) with open arms, a common gesture to express something **large**.

6. 山 (Shān) Mountain.

Note: Pictogram of a **mountain** with three peaks.

7. 水 (Shuǐ) Water.

Note: Pictogram of a stream of **water** in the center with drops splashing on the sides. When it is part of another character, its writing is simplified as 氵.

8. 月 (Yuè) Month, Moon.

Note: Pictogram of the crescent **moon**, it is also the simplified character of meat.

The Logic of Chinese Characters

9. 木 (Mù) Tree, wood.

Note: Pictogram of a **tree**.

10. 女 (Nǚ) Woman, female.

Note: Pictogram of a **woman** walking with outstretched arms.
- 女人 Woman: 女 (Woman) + 人 (Person)

11. 火 (Huǒ) Fire.

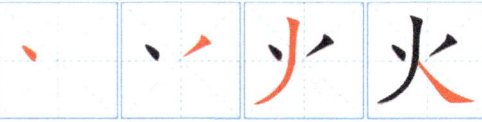

Note: Pictogram of **fire** flames. When it is part of another character, its writing is simplified as 灬.
- 火山 Volcano: 火 (Fire) + 山 (Mountain).

12. 力 (Lì) Force, power, Strength.

Note: Pictogram of a plowing tool, which required a lot of **force**.

The Logic of Chinese Characters

13. 马 (Mǎ) Horse.

Note: Simplified pictogram of a **horse**.

14. 目 (Mù) Eye.

Note: Pictogram of a person's **eye** rotated 90 degrees to a vertical position.

15. 手 (Shǒu) Hand.

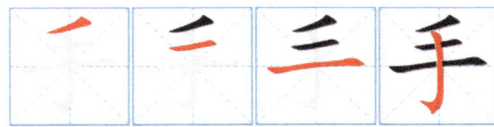

Note: Pictogram of a **hand**. When it is part of another character, its writing is usually simplified as 扌.

16. 太 (Tài) Greatest, hightest.

Note: Pictogram of a large person (大) riding on a stone to indicate something **extremely** larger. See character no. 5.

17. 门 (Mén) Door, gate.

<u>Note:</u> Pictogram of an open **door**.
- 门口 Door, entrance: 门 (Door) + 口 (Mouth).

18. 工 (Gōng) Work, Worker.

<u>Note:</u> Pictogram of a tool used for **work**.
- 木工 Carpenter: 木 (Wood) + 工 (Work).
- 手工 Craft, handmade: 手 (Hand) + 工 (Work).

19. 开 (Kāi) Open, turn on.

<u>Note:</u> Pictogram of an open **door**.
- 开门 Open the door: 开 (Open) + 门 (Door).

20. 关 (Guān) Close, turn off.

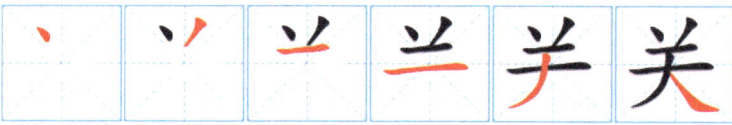

<u>Note:</u> Pictogram of a **closed** door.
- 关门 Close the door: 关 (Close) + 门 (Door).

The Logic of Chinese Characters

21. 田 (Tián) Field, farmland.

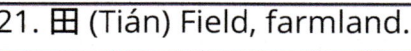

Note: Pictogram of a rice **field**.

22. 男 (Nán) Man, male.

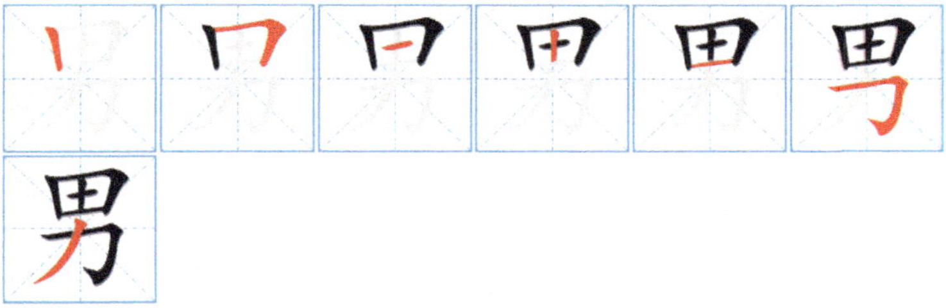

Note: Associative character of Field (田) and Strength (力), in antiquity generally those who worked in the fields were **men** due to their physical strength. See character no. 12 and 21.

23. 上 (Shàng) Up, upper, above, on.

Note: Indicative character, it suggests something that is located **above** the base. See character no. 24.

24. 下 (Xià) Down, downward, under.

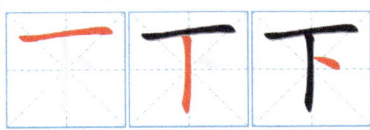

Note: Indicative character, it suggests something that is located **below** the base. See character no. 23.

25. 明 (Míng) Bright, Light.

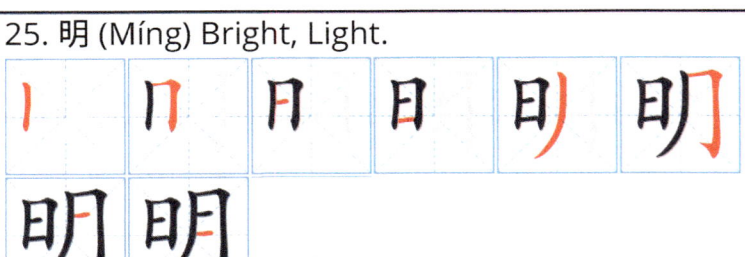

Note: Associative character of Sun (日) and Moon (月), The two sources of natural **light**. See character no. 3 and 8.

26. 们(Men) Suffix indicating plural, used after the pronoun or certain nouns.

Note: Picto-phonetic character of Person (人=亻) and Door (门), the left side (人) gives a semantic connotation of **several people**. The right side (门=Mén) a phonetic, in order to be an aid to remember its pronunciation. See character no. 1 and 17.

27. 几 (Jǐ) How many? Several, a few.

Note: Pictogram of a table, where you can place a few small things to **count** them.

28. 心 (Xīn) Heart.

Note: Pictogram or visual representation of the human **heart**. When it is part of another character, its simplified form is 忄.

The Logic of Chinese Characters

29. 天 (Tiān) Sky, day.

Note: Ideographic character that represents the **sky** by indicating that there is something higher than a big person (大). See character no. 5.
- 明天 Tomorrow: 明 (Bright) + 天 (Day).

30. 了 (Le) Time particle that indicates the change of a situation or the end of it. (Liǎo) Understand, absolutely.

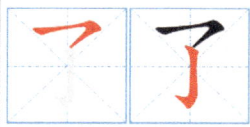

Note: Simplified pictogram, originally this character represented the image of a newborn baby with the head downwards. This explanation is in harmony with its current meaning, which is a particle indicating the **conclusion or change in an action**. The current form of the character has undergone simplifications over time and no longer visually reflects the original representation of a newborn baby.

31. 飞 (Fēi) Fly.

Note: Pictogram of a bird **flying**, with wings spread.

The Logic of Chinese Characters

32. 子 (Zǐ) Child, son, Diminutive suffix for objects.

Note: Simplified pictogram, originally this character looks like a stylized representation of a **baby** (了) in a fetal position. See character no. 30.

33. 字 (Zì) Escritura, carácter, palabra.

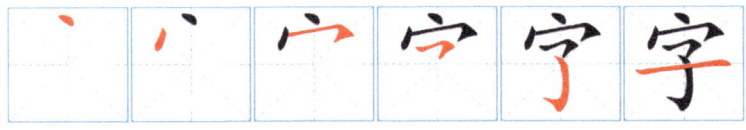

Note: Associative character of Child (子) and roof (宀), ideogram of a child under a roof with the possibility of education, or learning **writing**. See character no. 30 and 32.

34. 不 (Bù) Not, deny.

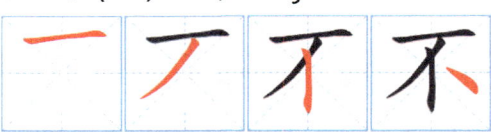

Note: Simplified pictogram of a plant growing downwards, something that was considered improbable and the representation of **denial**.

35. 小 (Xiǎo) Small, little.

Note: Pictogram of a **small** sprout emerging from the ground.
- 小心 Be careful, caution: 小 (Small) + 心 (Heart).

The Logic of Chinese Characters

36. 王 (Wáng) King, monarch.

Note: Simplified pictogram of a crown, which is usually placed on the head of a **king**.

37. 学 (Xué) Learn, study.

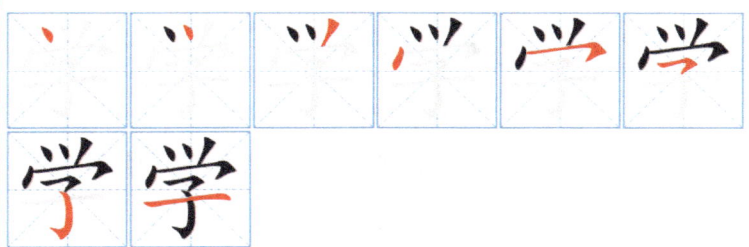

Note: Associative character of boy (子) with a crown on his head, indicating the act of **studying and learning**. See character no. 30 and 32.
- 大学 University: 大 (Big) + 学 (Study).

38. 在 (Zài) Be at, in.

Note: Associative character of hand (手 = 扌) in a simplified form and ground (土). A hand taking the ground indicating **presence in a territory**. See character no. 4 and 15.

The Logic of Chinese Characters

39. 有 (Yǒu) To have.

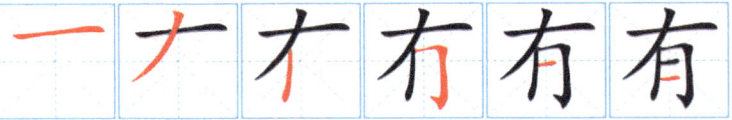

<u>Note:</u> Associative character of hand (手 = 扌) in a simplified form and Moon (月). A hand holding the moon indicating **possession** of something. See character no. 4 and 8.

40. 中 (Zhōng) Center, middle, in the middle.

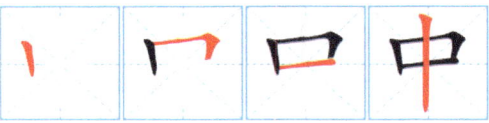

<u>Note:</u> Indicative character visual representation of the **center** of something.

41. 我 (Wǒ) I, personal pronoun.

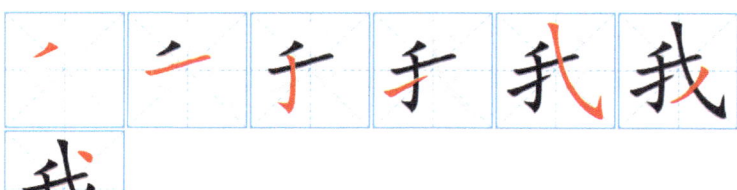

<u>Note:</u> Simplified pictogram of a hand (手 = 扌) holding a weapon, which could indicate the action of assuming command in the middle of a battle by saying "**Me**". See character no. 15.
- 我们 We: 我 (I) + 们 (suffix indicating plural).

42. 个 (Gè) General use measurement word.

Note: Simplified pictogram, some versions indicate that it is an arrow **pointing to** a person. See character no. 1.

43. 果 (Guǒ) Fruit, result.

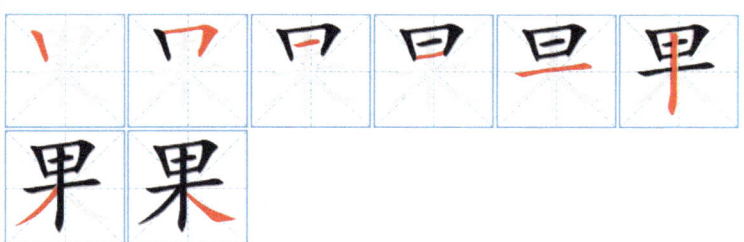

Note: Associative character formed by the pictograms of "field" (田) and "Tree" (木). This ideogram represents the image of a tree planted in cultivated land, symbolizing the idea of a tree that produces **fruit**. See character no. 9 and 21.
- 水果 Fruit: 水 (Water) + 果 (fruit).

44. 也 (Yě) Also, too, neither.

Note: This character has evolved from older versions that had the shape of a hand extended forward or an arm with an open hand. In a broader context, this representation could suggest the idea of reaching out and taking something, which has been associated with the modern meaning of "**too**."

The Logic of Chinese Characters

45. 他 (Tā) He, personal pronoun.

Note: Associative character of Person (人=亻) and Also (也), it is used to indicate that the human figure represents **another person** besides the speaker. See character no. 1 and 44.
- 他们 They: 他 (He) + 们 (suffix indicating plural).

46. 她 (Tā) She, personal pronoun.

Note: Associative character of Woman (女) and Also (也), it is used to indicate that the figure of a woman represents **another person**, in addition to the speaker. See character no. 10 and 44.
- 她们 Ellas: 她 (She) + 们 (suffix indicating plural).

47. 地 (dì) Earth, soil, location. (de) Particle placed before the verb to indicate adverb

Note: Associative character of Land (土) and Also (也), to indicate that the **earth** represents an extensive surface and also a specific place or location. See character no. 4 and 44.
- 地下 Underground: 地 (Soil) + 下 (Down).
- 土地 Soil, Lands: 土 (Land) + 地 (Soil).

The Logic of Chinese Characters

48. 好 (Hǎo) Well, good.

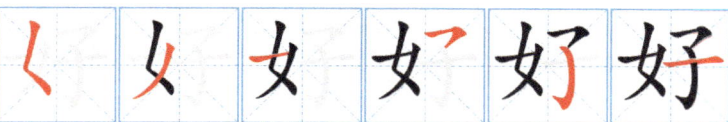

Note: Associative character of a woman (女) with her young son (子) representing what is considered good or appropriate. See character no. 10 and 32.
- 好心 Kind: 好 (Good) + 心 (Heart).

49. 见 (Jiàn) See, Look.

Note: Simplified pictogram of an eyebrow above the eye, symbolizing the action of **looking or seeing**.

50. 主 (Zhǔ) Owner, host, Sir.

Note: Associative character of King (王) with a stroke above, this stroke (丶) can represent a pole or a focal point. It conveys the idea of someone who is watching over **his property or land**. See character no. 36.
- 主人 Owner: 主 (Owner) + 人 (Person).
- 天主 Lord of heaven, God: 天 (Heaven) + 主 (Lord).
- 地主 Landowner: 地 (Land) + 主 (Owner).

The Logic of Chinese Characters

51. 生 (Shēng) Life, birth, new, unknown, raw.

<u>Note:</u> Pictogram of a sprout that **grows** from the ground.
- 学生 Student: 学 (Study) + 生 (Life).
- 生日 Birthday: 生 (Birth) + 日 (Day).
- 人生 Human life: 人 (Person) + 生 (Life).

52. 本 (Běn) Root, base, measurement word for books.

<u>Note:</u> Indicative character, pictogram of a tree (木) with a horizontal line indicating its **root**. See character no. 9.
- 本子 Notebook: 本 (measurement word for books) + 子 (child).
- 日本 Japan: 日 (Sun) + 本 (root).

53. 里 (Lǐ) Inside, inner, within.

<u>Note:</u> Associative character of Territory (土) and field (田), indicating the crop fields that are **within** the farmers' territories. When it is part of another character, its simplified form is 阝 and represents being **inside** a city or a mountain. See character no. 4, 6 and 21.
- 心里 Inside the heart, in the heart: 心 (Heart) + 里 (Within).

25

54. 足 (Zú) Foot.

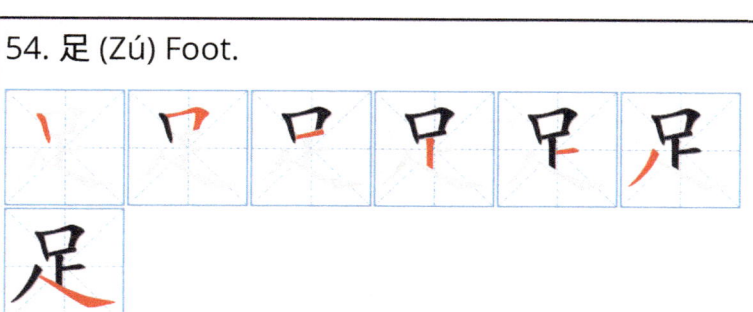

<u>Note:</u> Simplified pictogram of a **foot**. When it is part of another character, its simplified form is 夂.

55. 从 (Cóng) Follow, from, Since.

<u>Note:</u> Associative character of a person (人) **following** another person. See character no. 1.
- 从不 Never: 从 (Since) + 不 (No).
- 从小 Since childhood: 从 (Since) + 小 (Little).

56. 头 (Tóu) Head, hair, beginning, top.

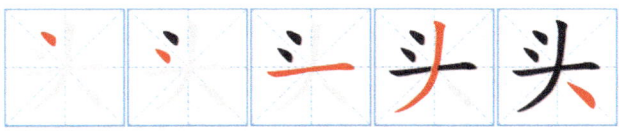

<u>Note:</u> Pictogram of a man's (人) **head** with **hair** floating in the wind. See character no. 1.
- 开头 Start: 开 (Open) + 头 (Beginning).
- 山头 Mountain summit: 山 (mountain) + 头 (Head).

57. 是 (Shì) Verb to be, right.

Note: Indicative character of a person walking represented by the character of foot (足) under the sun (日) with nothing to hide, **being correct**. See character no. 3 and 54.

58. 电 (Diàn) Electricity.

Note: Pictogram of **lightning** crossing a field. See character number 21.
- 电工 Electrician: 电 (Electricity) + 工 (Work).
- 电力 Electrical energy: 电 (Electricity) + 力 (Strength).

59. 少 (Shǎo) Little, few, less, missing.

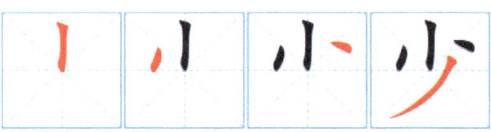

Note: Ideogram with extended meaning that represents the **few** sprouts of a soybean plant.
- 少见 Rare, difficult to see: 少 (Little) + 见 (See).
- 少女 Young girl: 少 (Little) + 女 (Woman).

60. 儿 (Ér) Son.

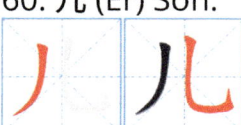

Note: Simplified pictogram, in its earliest versions it was the ideogram of a **child**, currently it is a more simplified one with only two strokes.
- 儿子 Son: 儿 (Son) + 子 (Child).
- 女儿 Daughter: 女 (Woman) + 儿 (Son).

61. 走 (Zǒu) Leave, go, walk.

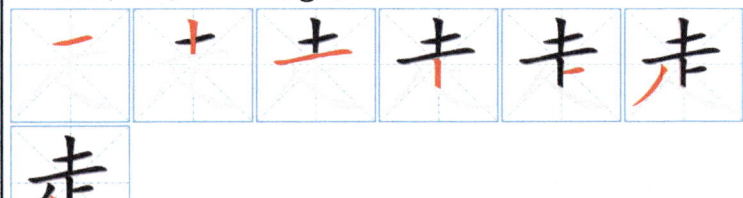

Note: Associative character of Earth (土) and Foot (足), indicating a movement from one territory to another, **walking, leaving**. When it is part of another character, its writing is simplified as 辶. See character no. 4 and 54.
- 飞走 Fly away: 飞 (Fly) + 走 (Leave).

62. 机 (Jī) Machine, engine.

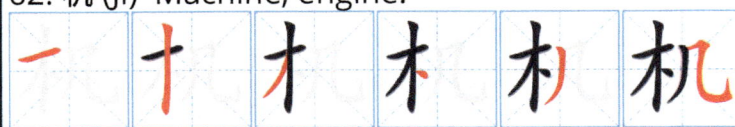

Note: Associative character of Tree (木) and Some (几), indicating the joining of a few trees to form a **machine** or a weapon, a practice used in ancient times. See character no. 9 and 27.
- 手机 Mobile phone: 手 (Hand) + 机 (Machine).
- 飞机 Airplane: 飞 (Fly) + 机 (Machine).
- 关机 Turn off the machine: 关 (Turn off) + 机 (Machine).

63. 白 (Bái) White color.

Note: Pictographic indicative character of a **white** candle, the light coming from a candle reflected by the character for sun (日) with a stroke at the top. See character no. 3.
- 白人 White person: 白 (White) + 人 (Person).
- 明白 Understand: 明 (Bright) + 白 (White).

64. 实 (Shí) True, reality, fact.

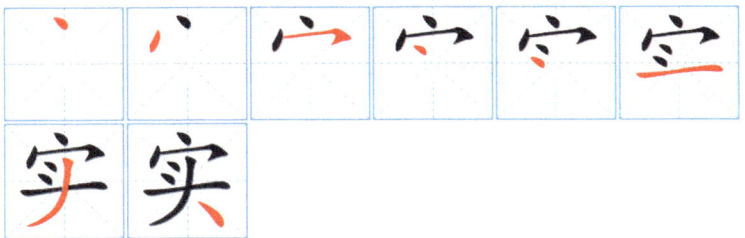

Note: Associative character of head (头) and roof (宀), indicating a person under the roof of their own house, feeling **real security, a fact**. See character no. 56.
- 实在 Real fact: 实 (True) + 在 (Be in).

65. 寸 (Cùn) Inch (measurement word).

Note: Simplified pictogram, Originally it was represented with a hand with the thumb extended indicating this **unit of measurement.**

66. 玉 (Yù) Jade stone.

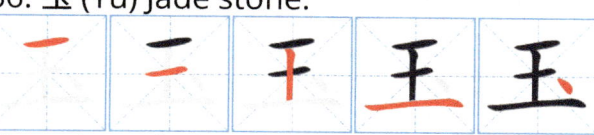

Note: Associative character of a King (王) with a **jade** precious stone in his clothing. See character no. 36.

67. 国 (Guó) State, country, nation.

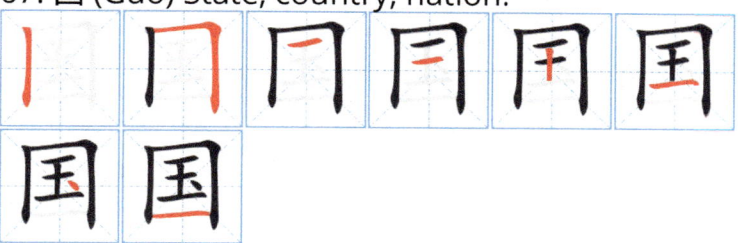

Note: Associative character of a jade stone (玉) protected by guarded borders, which conveys the idea of a **country or nation**. See character no. 66.

68. 长 (Cháng) Grow, long, (zhǎng) Seem, Old man, elder.

Note: Simplified pictogram of the face of an older man with long, abundant hair, representing **old age**.
- 长大 Grow: 长 (Grow) + 大 (Big).

69. 刀 (Dāo) Knife, knife-shaped object.

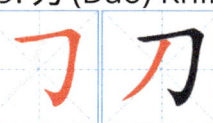

Note: Pictogram of a **knife** used in ancient times. When it is part of another character, its simplified form is 刂.
- 开刀 Perform or undergo an operation: 开 (Open) + 刀 (Knife).

The Logic of Chinese Characters

70. 文 (Wén) Writing, character, text, written language.

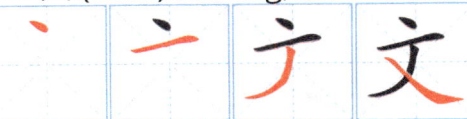

Note: Simplified pictogram of a person **with tattoos** on their chest, now it is just a person highlighting the chest area.
- 文学 Literature: 文 (Writing) + 学 (Study).
- 中文 Chinese Language: 中 (Center) + 文 (Writing).

71. 这 (Zhè) This These.

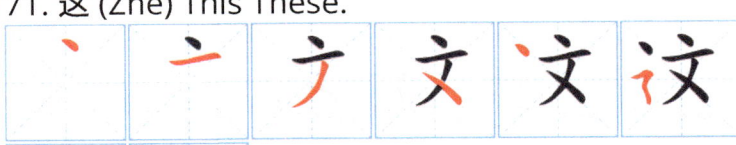

Note: Associative character of leaving (走=辶) and Writing (文), it symbolizes **sending a word to point out something or someone**. See character no. 61 and 70.
- 这里 Here: 这 (East) + 里 (Within).
- 这个 East: 这 (East) + 个 (Measure word for things).
- 这人 This person: 这 (This) + 人 (Person).

72. 来 (Lái) To come, to arrive.

Note: Pictogram of a wheat plant that represents the **arrival** of the harvest.
- 上来 Up here: 上 (Up) + 来 (come).
- 从来 From the past until now, always: 从 (From) + 来 (come).

73. 时 (Shí) Time, hour, time period.

Note: Associative character of day (日) and inch (寸), the inches or measurements of the day are **hours, time**. See character no. 3 and 65.
- 小时 Time: 小 (Small) + 时 (Time).
- 有时 Sometimes: 有(Have) + 时 (Time).

74. 为 (Wèi) For, in order to. (wéi) Do, act like, become.

Note: Associative character of Force (力) and two strokes indicating movement, the force in motion **for a** specific purpose. See character no. 12.
- 为生 Make a living: 为 (In order to) + 生 (life).

75. 后 (Hòu) Afterwards, after, later, back, descendant.

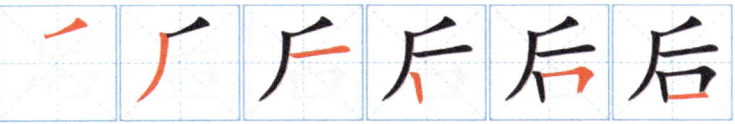

Note: Pictogram of a woman giving birth to the next generation. See character no. 2.
- 后人 Future generations: 后 (After) + 人 (Person).
- 后来 Then, later: 后 (After) + 来 (Come).
- 后天 The day after tomorrow: 后 (After) + 天 (Day).
- 王后 Queen: 王 (King) + 后 (Back).

The Logic of Chinese Characters

76. 而 (Ér) However, but, as well as, and, so as.

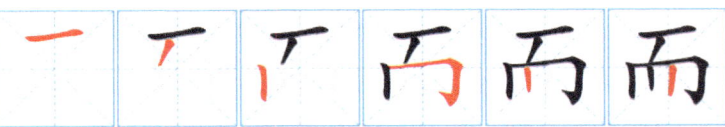

<u>Note:</u> Character with extended meaning. Pictogram of a face with a mustache and beard of an older man.
- 从而 Therefore: 从 (Since) + 而 (So as).

77. 又 (Yòu) Again, on the other hand, and.

<u>Note:</u> Character with extended sense of the right hand, indicating to do something again.

78. 过 (Guò) Pass, cross, exceed, error, mistake, past action suffix.

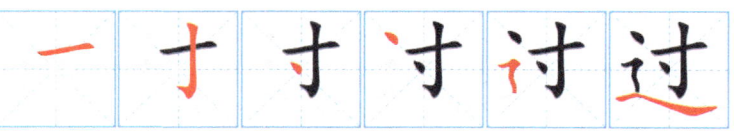

<u>Note:</u> Associative character of leave (走=辶) and inch (寸) indicating retreat a distance measured in inches. See character no. 61 and 65.
- 过来 Come: 过 (Pass) + 来 (Come).
- 过关 Overcome a barrier: 过 (Pass) + 关 (close).
- 看过 Having seen: 看 (See) + 过 (Past action).

79. 相 (Xiāng) Mutually, reciprocal, aspect, appearance.

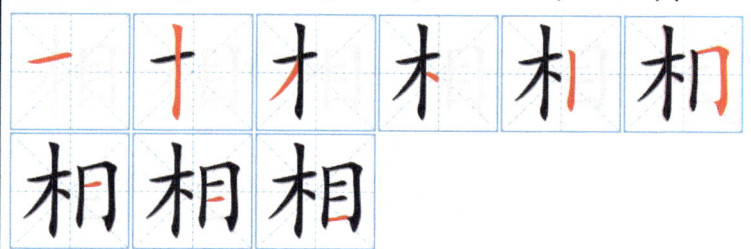

Note: Associative character of "tree" (木) and "eye" (目) giving the idea of an eye observing the **appearance** of a tree. See character no. 9, 14.
- 相机 Camera: 相 (Appearance) + 机 (Machine).
- 相见 Meet: 相 (Mutually) + 见 (See).
- 长相 Appearance, aspect: 长 (Look) + 相 (mutually).

80. 云 (Yún) Cloud.

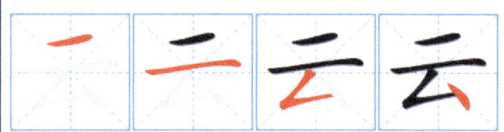

Note: Simplified pictogram of **clouds**.
- 白云 White clouds: 白 (White) + 云 (Cloud).
- 少云 Little cloudy: 少 (Little) + 云 (Cloud).

81. 用 (Yòng) Use, employ, apply.

Note: Pictogram of a crop field (田) being harvested, that is, **used**. See character no. 21.
- 好用 Practical, easy to use: 好 (Good) + 用 (Use).

82. 友 (Yǒu) Friend, friendship.

Note: Associative character of two hands (手 = 扌) and (又) shaking, exemplifying friendship. See character no. 15 and 77.
- 男友 Boyfriend: 男 (Man) + 友 (Friendship).
- 女友 Girlfriend: 女 (Woman) + 友 (Friendship).
- 工友 Coworker: 工 (Work) + 友 (Friendship).

83. 牛 (Niú) Ox, cow, bull, buffalo, animals similar to an Ox.

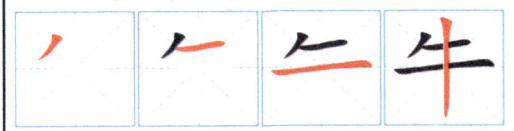

Note: Pictogram of the head of an **Ox** from which one horn has been removed.
- 小牛 Calf: 小 (Small) + 牛 (Cow).
- 水牛 Water buffalo: 水 (Water) + 牛 (buffalo).

84. 出 (Chū) Go out, emerge, produce, exit.

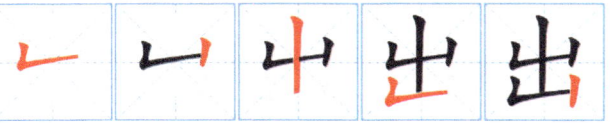

Note: Pictogram of one mountain (山) **emerging** from another. See character no. 6.
- 出走 Run away, escape: 出 (Go out) + 走 (Leave).
- 出生 Birth: 出 (Exit) + 生 (Life).
- 出国 Go abroad: 出 (Go out) + 国 (Country).

85. 以 (Yǐ) In order to, with, through, according to.

<u>Note:</u> Pictogram of a person (人) carrying their belongings to go on a mission. See character no. 1.
- 以后 After: 以 (According to) + 后 (After).

86. 去 (Qù) Go, go to.

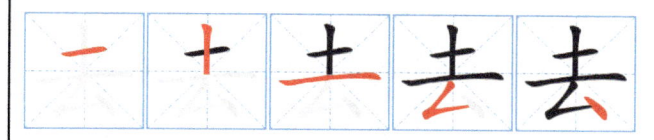

<u>Note:</u> Associative character of a territory (土) above a cloud (云) **going** somewhere. See character no. 4 and 80.
- 上去 Go up: 上 (Up) + 去 (Go).
- 下去 Go down: 下 (Down) + 去 (Go).

87. 于 (Yú) In, on, at, to.

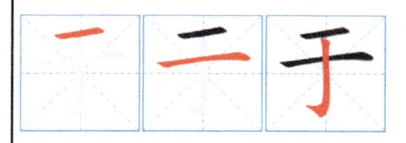

<u>Note:</u> Pictogram of a musical instrument.
- 用于 Use in, use for: 用 (Use) + 于 (In).
- 出于 Because of, come from: 出 (Go out) + 于 (To).
- 关于 About, in relation to: 关 (Close) + 于 (To).

88. 现 (Xiàn) Now, present, show, appear.

Note: Picto-phonetic character of a king (王) **coming into view** (见). The character on the right (见=Jiàn) also serves a phonetic function as a reminder of its pronunciation. See character no. 36 and 49.
- 现在 Now, at this moment: 现 (Now) + 在 (Be at).
- 出现 Appear, arise: 出 (Exit) + 现 (appear).
- 现有 currently have, currently exist: 现 (Now) + 有 (Have).

89. 回 (Huí) Return, come back, answer, reply.

Note: Associative character of one mouth (口) **responding** to another forming a spiral. See character no. 2.
- 回来 Return, return: 回 (Return) + 来 (Come).
- 回去 Go again: 回 (Return) + 去 (Go).

90. 理 (Lǐ) Reason, logic, manage, law.

Note: Picto-phonetic character about what is expected of a king (王): That within (里) him, there is **logic and reason**. The character on the right (里 = Lǐ) also serves a phonetic function as a reminder of its pronunciation. See character no. 36 and 53.
- 不理 Ignore: 不 (No) + 理 (Manage).
- 有理 Reasonable: 有 (Have) + 理 (Reason).

91. 一 (Yī) One, First, 1.

Note: Indicative character of a horizontal line indicating **a unit**.
- 一月 January: 一 (One) + 月 (Month).
- 一日 One day: 一 (One) + 日 (Day).

92. 二 (Èr) Two, Second, 2.

Note: Indicative character of two horizontal lines indicating **two units**.
- 二手 Second-hand: 二 (Two) + 手 (Hand).
- 二月 February: 二 (Two) + 月 (Month).

93. 三 (Sān) Three, Third, 3.

Note: Indicative character of three horizontal lines indicating **three units**.
- 三天 Three days: 三 (Three) + 天 (Day).
- 三月 March: 三 (Three) + 月 (Month).

94. 四 (Sì) Four, fourth, 4.

Note: Pictogram of the nostrils, this is because n ancient times it was believed that the **number four** sounded the same as breathing.
- 四月 April: 四 (Four) + 月 (Month).
- 四口人 Four family members: 四 (Four) + 口 (measurement word for family members) + 人 (Person).

The Logic of Chinese Characters

95. 五 (Wǔ) Five, fifth, 5.

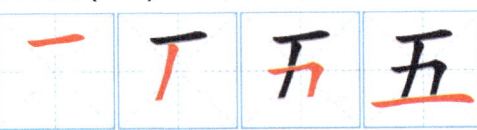

一　丆　乛　五

Note: Pictogram of a road with **five** exits.
- 五月 May: 五 (Five) + 月 (Month).

96. 六 (Liù) Six, sixth, 6.

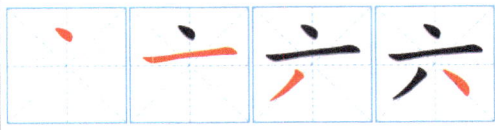

丶　亠　六　六

Note: Simplified pictogram of a roof of a typical ancient Chinese **six**-room house.
- 六月 June: 六 (Six) + 月 (Month).

97. 七 (Qī) Seventh, seven, 7.

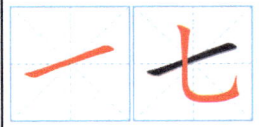

一　七

Note: indicative character of the number **seven**.

98. 八 (Bā) Eighth, eight, 8.

丿　八

Note: Indicative character of the number **Eight**.

99. 九 (Jiǔ) Nine, ninth, 9.

丿　九

Note: Indicative character of the number **Nine**, by adding a one (一) to the number eight (八). See character no. 91 and 98.

100. 十 (Shí) Ten, tenth, 10.

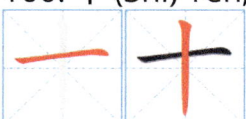

Note: Indicative character of the number **ten**, it represents perfection, something complete.

101. 自 (Zì) Oneself, self.

Note: Character with an extended sense of an eye (目) with one more stroke indicating the nose, which one usually points to when referring to **oneself**. See character no. 14.
- 自学 Learn oneself: 自 (Self) + 学 (Learn).
- 自在 Free, without restriction: 自 (Self) + 在 (Be in).
- 自大 Arrogant: 自 (Self) + 大 (Big).

102. 斤 (Jīn) Axe, Jin (Chinese weight measure approx. 500gr)

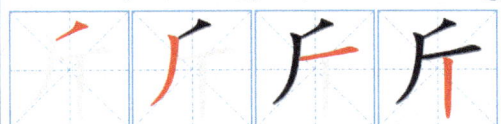

Note: Pictogram of an **ax** used in ancient times.

103. 可 (Kě) Able, can, may, approve, be willing to.

Note: Associative character of a mouth (口) and an ax (斤) indicating a **capable** person, who **can** find food and survive. See character no. 2 and 102.
- 可以 Can, may (permission to do something): 可 (Approve) + 以 (In order to).
- 可是 But: 可 (Can) + 是 (Being).
- 可口 Delicious: 可 (be willing to) + 口 (Mouth).

104. 对 (Duì) Correct, respond, opposite, oppose, reply.

Note: Associative character of a hand (又) measuring inches (寸) to confirm that it is **correct**. See character no. 65 and 77.
- 不对 Incorrect, wrong: 不 (No) + 对 (Correct).
- 对门 The door (neighbor) opposite: 对 (Opposite) + 门 (Door).
- 对手 Opponent, adversary: 对 (Oppose) + 手 (Hand).

105. 分 (Fēn) Divide, separate, distribute, Minute, points.

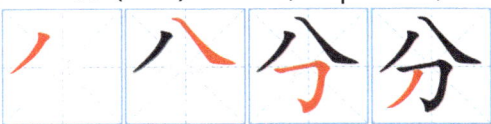

Note: Associative character of a knife (刀) **dividing** something into eight (八) pieces to **distribute** it. See character no. 69 and 98.
- 分开 Separate, divide: 分 (Separate) + 开 (Open).
- 分手 break up a relationship: 分 (Separate) + 手 (Hand).
- 分心 Distract, divert attention: 分 (Separate) + 心 (Heart).

106. 看 (Kàn) See, look, read.

Note: Associative character of a hand (手=扌) grabbing an eye (目) indicating the sense of **sight**. See character no. 14 and 15.
- 好看 Handsome, beautiful: 好 (Good) + 看 (See).
- 看见 See, see: 看 (Look) + 见 (See).
- 小看 Underestimate, view with contempt: 小 (Small) + 看 (See).

107. 方 (Fāng) Direction, side, region, place, square.

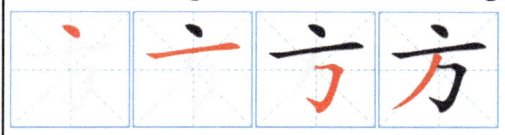

Note: Extended meaning character, Fang were a foreign tribe, continually enslaved as a result of wars. Ideogram of a man with a yoke on his neck.
- 地方 Place, site: 地 (Land) + 方 (Direction).
- 一方 One part: 一 (One) + 方 (Side).
- 对方 Opposite part: 对 (Opposite) + 方 (Side).

108. 成 (Chéng) Achieve, succeed, establish, become.

Note: Associative character of an ax (斤) crossing a line that indicates the border of a city, exemplifying its **successful** conquest. See character no. 102.
- 成果 Achievement: 成 (Achieve) + 果 (Fruit).
- 成为 Become: 成 (Become) + 为 (In order to).

109. 己 (Jǐ) Oneself, self.

Note: Pictogram of a rope, which was generally tied to the arrow to hunt birds, unlike other large animals that were distributed when hunted, hunting birds was to eat **oneself**.
- 自己 Oneself: 自 (Self) + 己 (Oneself).

110. 只 (Zhǐ) Only, just, merely, measurement word for birds and some animals.

Note: Associative character of a mouth (口) emitting various sounds, exemplified by the number eight (八), indicating the call of a bird trained for hunting that brought food **only** for its master.

111. 想 (Xiǎng) Want, think, imagine.

Note: Associative character of tree (木), eye (目) and heart (心). The union of these three characters conveys the idea of an eye seeing a tree and beginning to **think**, **imagine** and **desire** its fruit. See character no. 9, 14, 28.
- 心想 Thinking in the heart: 心 (Heart) + 想 (Thinking).
- 想来 Want to come: 想 (Want) + 来 (Come).

112. 问 (Wèn) Ask, question.

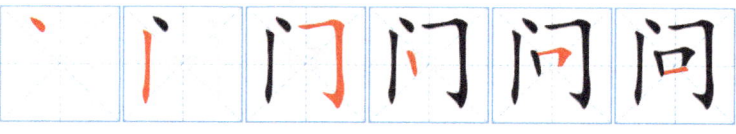

Note: Associative character of a mouth (口) on a door (门) **asking** for someone. See character no. 2 and 17.

113. 如 (Rú) Seem like, like, as if.

Note: Associative character of a mouth (口) Speaking **like** a woman (女). See character no. 2 and 10.
- 如果 If: 如 (As if) + 果 (Result).
- 如下 As indicated below: 如 (As if) + 下 (Down).

114. 还 (Hái) Still, yet, even more. (huán) return, back, give back.

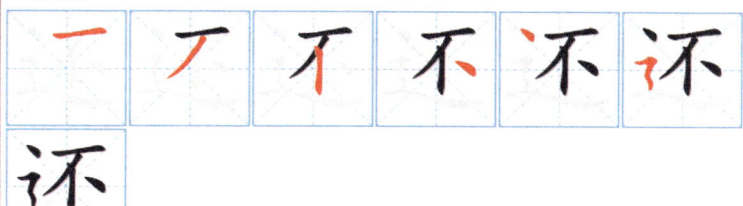

Note: Character indicative of someone who has nct (不) yet left (走=辶). See character no. 34 and 61.
- 还有 Still available: 还 (Still) + 有 (Have).
- 生还 Survive: 生 (Life) + 还 (Return).

115. 加 (Jiā) Add, sum, plus, increase.

Note: Associative character of a mouth (口) **Adding** comments with force (力). See character no. 2 and 12.
- 加时 Overtime, extra time: 加 (Add) + 时 (Time).
- 加大 Enlarge: 加 (Add) + 大 (Large).

116. 之 (Zhī) Possessive particle used in form language, to form a connection or relationship between words.

Note: Originally, it was a pictogram of a spear held upright.
- 之中 Within, between: 之 (Relation particle) + 中 (In the middle).

117. 风 (Fēng) Wind, style, custom.

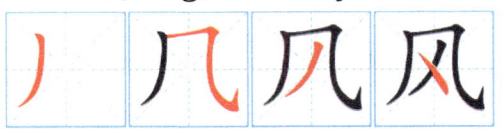

Note: Pictogram of a gust of wind seen from inside a cave.
- 风力 Wind strength: 风 (Wind) + 力 (Strength).

118. 么 (Me) Suffix used to formulate questions.

Note: Indicative nature, pictogram of a basket on someone's back, raising the **question**: What does it have inside?

119. 同 (Tóng) Identical, same, be equal to, together.

Note: Associative character of a door (冂) that fits into an exit (口) indicating that they are **the same** size. See character no. 2 and 17.
- 同学 Classmate: 同 (Together) + 学 (Study).
- 同时 At the same time: 同 (Same) + 时 (Time).
- 不同 Different: 不 (Not) + 同 (Identical).

120. 公 (Gōng) Public, common, collective, masculine.

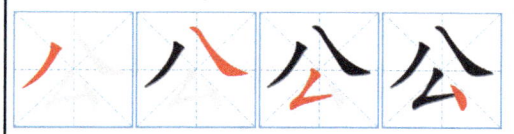

Note: Indicative character of eight (八) items in a basket for **public or collective** use. See character no. 98.
- 公斤 Kilo: 公 (Common) + 斤 (Jin).
- 公牛 Bull: 公 (Male) + 牛 (Ox).
- 公开 Make public: 公 (Public) + 开 (Open).

121. 入 (Rù) Enter, into, put in, entrance.

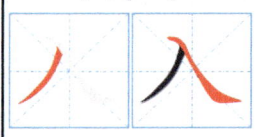

Note: Indicative character, pictogram of a person (人) bowing his head to **enter** a place. See character no. 1.
- 走入 Enter by walking: 走 (Walk) + 入 (Enter).
- 入口 Entrance door: 入 (Enter) + 口 (Mouth).

122. 体 (Tǐ) Body, substance, style, system.

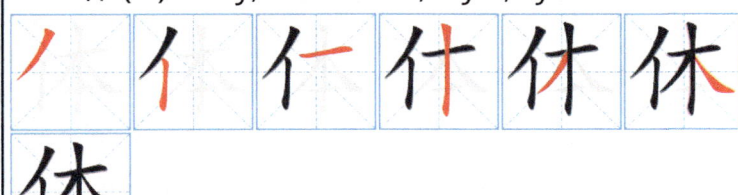

Note: Associative character of a person (人=亻) with his **body** represented by a tree (木) and its root (本). See character no. 1, 9 and 52.
- 字体 Font: 字 (Letter) + 体 (Style).
- 人体 Human body: 人 (Person) + 体 (Body).
- 体力 Physical strength: 体 (Body) + 力 (Strength).

123. 元 (Yuán) Boss, leader, principal, first, currency.

Note: Pictogram of a person with something on their head, indicating being the **leader**.

124. 全 (Quán) Completely, complete, whole, entire, full.

Note: Associative character of a king (王) entering (入) his palace indicating **absolute and complete** honor. See character no. 36 and 121.
- 全文 Full text: 全 (Full) + 文 (text).
- 全天 All day: 全 (Full) + 天 (day).

125. 没 (Méi) Not have, there is not, be without (mò) Sink, submerge.

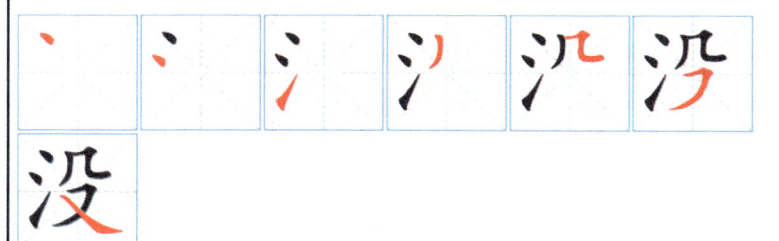

Note: Associative character of a hand (又) of a person **sinking** in water (水) after having fallen from a bridge, in this character represented by a table (几). See character no. 7, 27 and 77.
- 没去 Not have gone: 没 (Not have) + 去 (Go).
- 出没 Appear and disappear: 出 (Appear) + 没 (Disappear).

126. 动 (Dòng) Move, act, touch, use.

Note: Indicative character of the effect that the force (力) of the wind produces on a cloud (云), making it to **move**. See character no. 12 and 80.
- 动心 Emotion: 动 (Move) + 心 (Heart).
- 自动 Automatic: 自 (Self) + 动 (Move).
- 手动 Manual, manually operated: 手 (Hand) + 动 (Move).

127. 安 (Ān) Security, calm, tranquility.

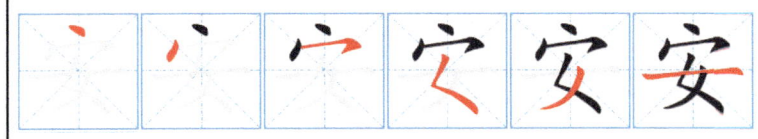

Note: Associative character of a woman (女) under a roof (宀) indicating a sense of **security and tranquility**. See character no. 10.
- 安全 Security: 安 (Security) + 全 (Complete).
- 不安 Uneasy: 不 (No) + 安 (Calm).

128. 广 (Guǎng) Wide, numerous, spread.

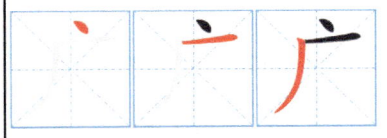

Note: Pictogram of a tree that has grown on the top of a **wide** plateau.

129. 法 (Fǎ) Law, method, form, model, magic.

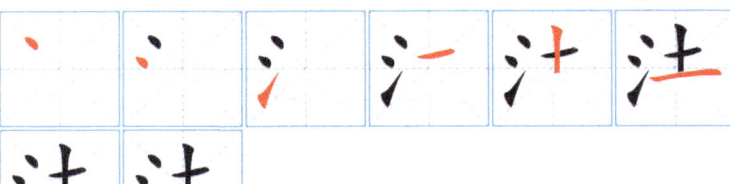

Note: Associative character that conveys the idea of going (去) to the side of the river, represented by water (水 = 氵) to practice a **form** of **magic**. See character no. 7 and 86.
- 方法 Method: 方 (Address) + 法 (Method).
- 看法 Point of view: 看 (See) + 法 (Form).
- 想法 Opinion: 想 (Think) + 法 (Form).

130. 厂 (Chǎng) Factory.

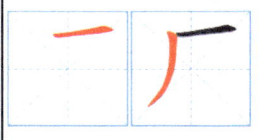

Note: Pictogram of a large warehouse (广) similar to a **factory**. See character no. 128.
- 工厂 Factory: 工 (Work) + 厂 (Factory).
- 厂长 Director of a factory: 厂 (Factory) + 长 (Elder).

131. 间 (Jiān) Room, space, time, between.

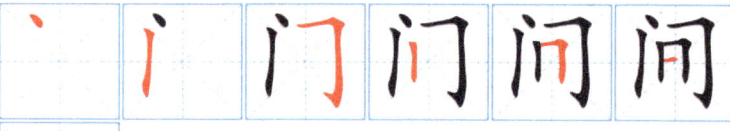

Note: Associative character of the sun (日) seen through a door (门) in a **room**. See character no. 3 and 17.
- 时间 Time period: 时 (Time) + 间 (space).

132. 区 (Qū) Zone, district, region, area.

Note: Simplified pictogram of a map of a **region**.
- 小区 zone, Urban complex: 小 (Small) + 区 (Zone).
- 地区 zone, area: 地 (Land) + 区 (Zone).
- 时区 time zone: 时 (Time) + 区 (Zone).

132. 言 (Yán) To speak, speech, say, word, sentence.

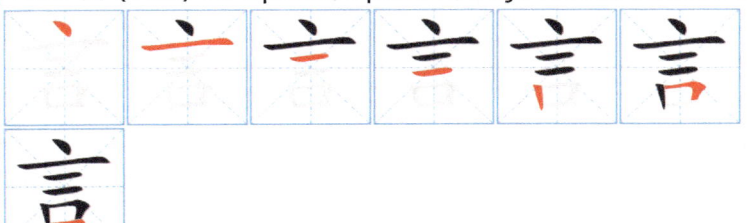

Note: Associative character of three (三) **words** coming out of a mouth (口). When it is part of another character, its writing is simplified as 讠. See character no. 2 and 93.
- 明言 Speak frankly: 明 (Bright) + 言 (Speech).
- 方言 Dialect: 方 (Place) + 言 (Word).

134. 发 (fā) Send, shoot, express. (fa) Hair.

Note: Pictogram of a person shooting an arrow.
- 发现 Discover, realize: 发 (Send) and 现 (Appear).
- 长发 Long hair: 长 (Long) + 发 (Hair).
- 发明 Invent: 发 (Send) + 明 (Bright).

135. 会 (Huì) Meet, see, know (do something), society, Particle of future. (Kuài) accounting.

Note: Associative character of a person (人) on top of a cloud (云) representing his great **knowledge** and **wisdom**. See character no. 1 and 80.
- 工会 Union: 工 (Work) + 会 (Society).
- 大会 Assembly: 大 (Big) + 会 (Meet).
- 开会 Start a meeting: 开 (Open) + 会 (Meet).

136. 民 (Mín) People, citizen, nation, folk, humanity.

Note: Indicative character of a person represented by a mouth (口) with an ax (斤) working, illustrating his active participation in **society** as a **citizen**. See character no. 2 and 102.
- 民主 Democracy: 民 (People) + 主 (Owner).
- 公民 Citizen: 公 (Collective) + 民 (Nation).
- 民用 For civil use: 民 (People) + 用 (Use).

137. 已 (Yǐ) Stop, finish, already.

Note: Simplified pictogram of a rope **stopping** something.

138. 因 (Yīn) Cause, reason, due to, because.

<u>Note:</u> Associative character of something big (大) coming out of a mouth (口) indicating someone who speaks **reasonably** or giving the **reason** for things. See character no. 2 and 5.
- 因为 Because, due to: 因 (Reason) + 为 (For).
- 因果 Cause and effect: 因 (Cause) + 果 (Result).
- 因而 Therefore, as a result: 因 (Cause) + 而 (So as).

139. 定 (Dìng) Stable, fix, secure, definitive.

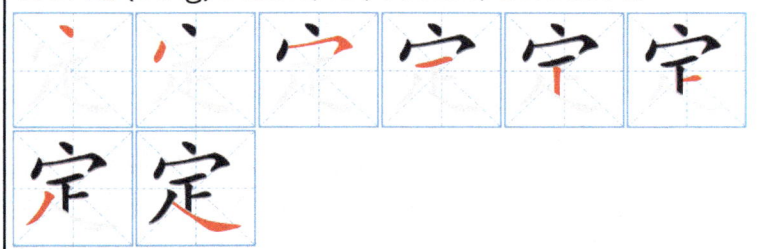

<u>Note:</u> Associative character of the foot (足) of a person arriving at his house, represented by a roof (宀), indicating a safe and **stable** place. See character no. 54.
- 一定 Without a doubt, definitely: 一 (One) + 定 (Definite).
- 安定 Calm, stable: 安 (Calm) + 定 (Stable).
- 法定 Legal, official: 法 (Law) + 定 (Stable).

140. 车 (Chē) Car, vehicle.

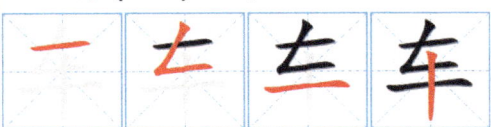

<u>Note:</u> Simplified pictogram of a **carriage**.
- 火车 Train: 火 (Fire) + 车 (Vehicle).
- 开车 Driving a car: 开 (Open) + 车 (Vehicle).
- 公车 Public transportation: 公 (Public) + 车 (Vehicle).

141. 办 (Bàn) Manage, execute, handle, process.

Note: Indicative character of a force tool (力) moving in order to **execute** work. See character no. 12.
- 办理 Manage a matter: 办 (Handle) + 理 (Manage).
- 办法 Way of resolving something: 办 (Handle) + 法 (Form).

142. 认 (Rèn) Know, recognize, identify, admit, accept.

Note: Associative character of a person (人) **recognizing or identifying** another by their way of speaking (言). See character no. 1 and 133.
- 公认 Generally accepted: 公 (Public) + 认 (Accept).
- 认可 Approve: 认 (Accept) + 为 (In orden to).
- 认为 Consider, opine: 认 (Recognize) + 为 (For).

143. 什 (Shén) What?

Note: Indicative character of one person (人=亻) in the middle of ten others (十) **asking** something. See character no. 1 and 100.
- 什么 What?: 什 (What?) + 么 (Question suffix).
- 为什么 Why?: 为 (For) + 什 (What?) + 么 (Question suffix).

144. 至 (Zhì) Arrive, reach, until, to.

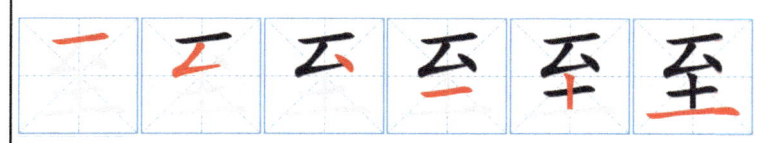

<u>Note:</u> Associative character of highlands (土) **reaching** a cloud (云). See character no. 4 and 80.
- 至少 At least: 至 (Until) + 少 (Few).
- 至上 Above all, supreme: 至 (Arrive) + 上 (Up).

145. 年 (Nián) Year.

<u>Note:</u> Indicative character of an ox (牛) being sacrificed on an altar, welcoming the new **year**. See character no. 83.
- 去年 Last year: 去 (Leave) + 年 (Year).
- 明年 The following year: 明 (Bright) + 年 (Year).
- 全年 All year: 全 (Full) + 年 (Year).

146. 勺 (Sháo) Spoon.

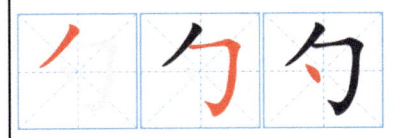

<u>Note:</u> Simplified pictogram of a spoon with content inside.
- 勺子 Spoon: 勺 (Spoon) + 子 (Diminutive suffix).

147. 到 (Dào) Arrive, reach, go out to, leave, to.

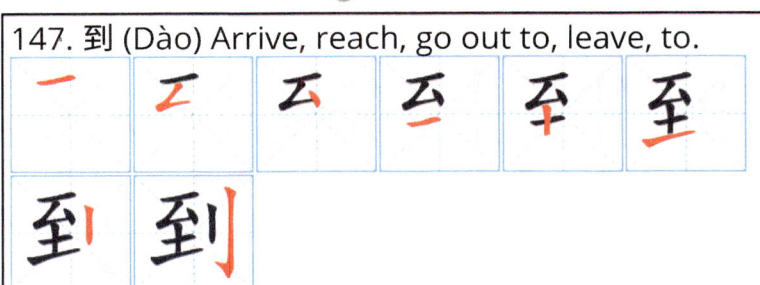

Note: Picto-phonetic character of "until" or "**arrive**" (至) and Knife (刀+ 刂), the left side 至 gives a semantic connotation, with the meaning very similar to 至. The right side (刀 = Dāo) a phonetic, in order to help remember its pronunciation. See character no. 69 and 144.

- 回到 Return, back: 回 (Return) + 到 (To).
- 走到 Walk to: 走 (Walk) + 到 (to).

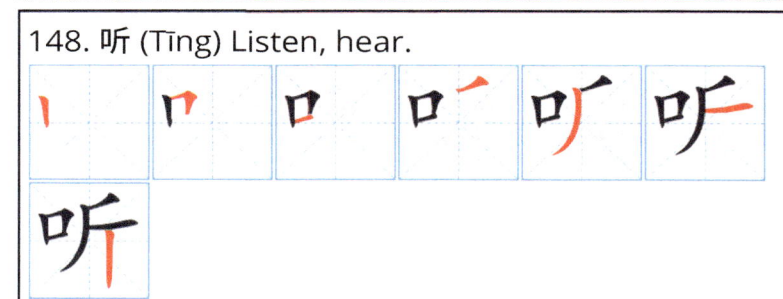

148. 听 (Tīng) Listen, hear.

Note: Associative character of a person, represented by a mouth (口) **listening** to the sound of an Ax (斤). See character no. 2 and 102.

- 听力 Hearing ability: 听 (Listen) + 力 (Strength).
- 好听 Melodious, pleasant to the ear: 好 (Good) + 听 (Listen).

149. 介 (Jiè) Situate between, mind, care.

Note: Pictogram of a person (人) located inside armor. See character no. 1.

- 介入 intervene, interpose: 介 (Interpose) + 入 (Enter).

150. 让 (Ràng) Leave, give in, allow, ask (someone to do something).

Note: Associative character of a word (言 = 讠) **asking** permission to upload (上). See character no. 23 and 133.
- 让开 Give way: 让 (Give) + 开 (Open).

151. 的 (De) Possessive particle. (Dì) objective.

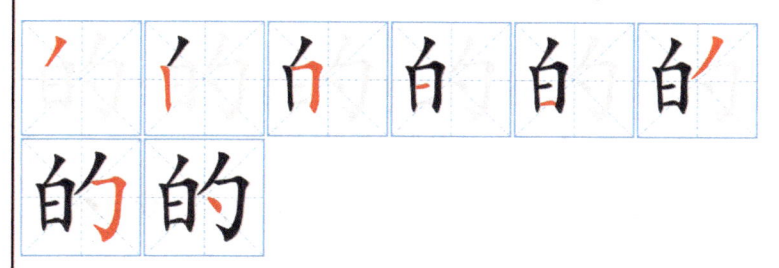

Note: Associative character of a spoon (勺) entering the mouth, which is its **objective**, represented by the color white (白). See character no. 63 and 146.
- 目的 Purpose, objective: 目 (Eye) + 的 (Objective).
- 我的 Mine, mine: 我 (I) + 的 (Possessive particle).

152. 干 (De) Work, do, dry.

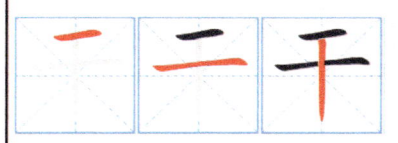

Note: Pictogram of a dry tree to make wood.
- 干果 Nuts: 干 (Dry) + 果 (Fruit).

153. 观 (Guān) Look, observe, view.

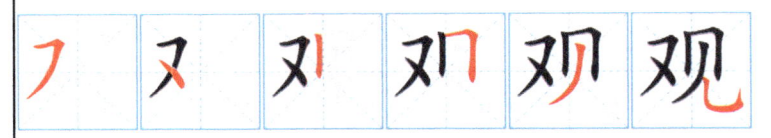

Note: Associative character of a hand (又) placed above the eyes to **look** (见) into the distance. See character no. 49 and 77.
- 观看 Observe: 观 (Observe) + 看 (See).

154. 众 (Zhòng) Crowd, many, multitude.

Note: Associative character of three people (人) together representing a **crowd**. See character no. 1.
- 观众 Spectator: 观 (Observe) + 众 (Crowd).
- 听众 Listening audience: 听 (Listen) + 众 (Crowd).
- 出众 Exceptional, out of the ordinary: 出 (Go out) + 众 (Crowd).

155. 石 (Shí) Stone, Rock.

Note: Pictogram of a **stone** falling from a wide cliff (广). See character no. 128.
- 玉石 Jade: 玉 (Jade) + 石 (Stone).

156. 林 (Lín) Forest, forester, woods.

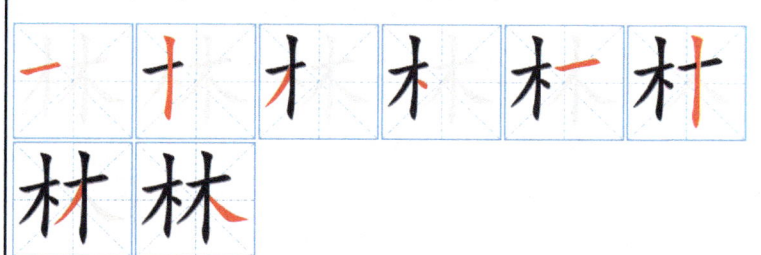

Note: Associative character of two trees (木), exemp ifying the birth of a **forest**. See character no. 9.
- 林区 Forest zone: 林 (Forest) + 区 (zone).

157. 平 (Píng) Flat, smooth, level, plain, uniform, fair, calm.

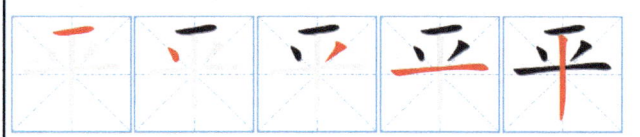

Note: Pictogram of a scale measuring two exactly **uniform** weights.
- 水平 Level: 水 (Water) + 平 (Level).
- 平地 Plain: 平 (Plain) + 地 (Land).
- 平手 Tie: 平 (Uniform) + 手 (Hand).

158. 禾 (Hé) Cereal, grain.

Note: Pictogram of an ear of **grain** with the upper stroke curved due to the weight of the grain.

159. 羊 (Yáng) Sheep, goat.

Note: Pictogram of a **goat** with two large horns.
- 山羊 Goat: 山 (Montana) + 羊 (Goat).
- 一只羊 A sheep: 一 (One) + 只 (Measure word) + 羊 (Sheep).

160. 内 (Nèi) Internal, inside, within.

Note: Associative character of a person (人) accessing the **interior** of a house by entering through the door (门). See character no. 1 and 17.
- 国内 Interior of a country: 国 (Country) + 内 (Interior).
- 以内 Inside: 以 (Through) + 内 (Inside).

161. 和 (Hé) And, along with, peace, harmony.

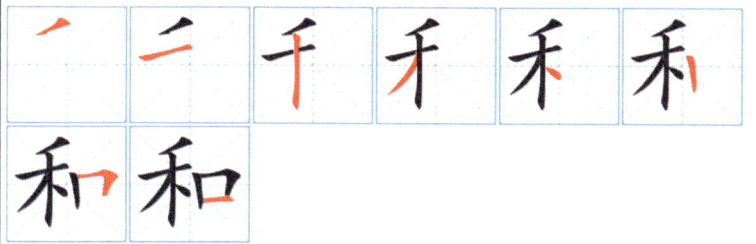

Note: Picto-phonetic character of cereal (禾) and Mouth (口), the left side (禾=Hé) gives a phonetic connotation in order to help remember its pronunciation. The right side 口 a semantics. Mouths singing the arrival of the harvest, a song that was made between two people in a **harmonious** way. See character no. 2 and 158.
- 和平 Peace: 和 (Peace) + 平 (Calm).
- 和好 Reconcile: 和 (Harmonious) + 好 (Good).

The Logic of Chinese Characters

162. 由 (Yóu) Cause, reason, follow, way, through.

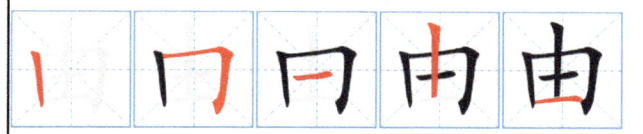

<u>Note:</u> Associative character of a path **through** the crop field (田). See character no. 21.
- 自由 Freedom: 自 (Self) + 由 (Reason).
- 由来 Origin: 由 (Follow) + 来 (Arrive).

163. 品 (Pǐn) Article, product, item, class, quality.

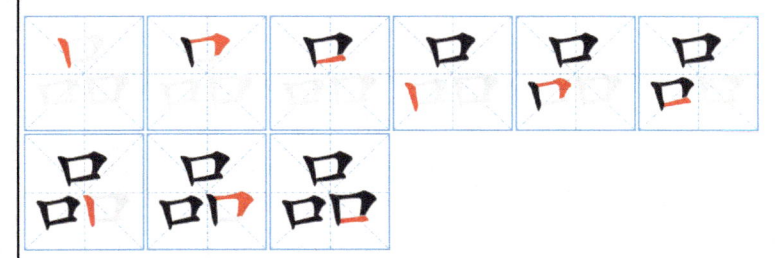

<u>Note</u>: Pictogram of three stacked items.
- 日用品 Daily Use Item: 日 (Day) + 用 (Use) + 品 (Item).

164. 丁 (Dīng) Man doing manual work.

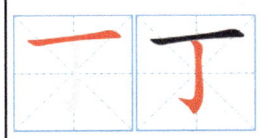

<u>Note</u>: Pictogram of a nail, indicating a person who performs manual labor.

165. 面 (Miàn) Face, side, surface, flour, noodles.

Note: Character indicative of a nose (自) with forehead and cheeks on both sides forming a **face**. See character no. 101.
- 见面 Meeting someone: 见 (See) + 面 (Face).
- 里面 Inner side: 里 (Inside) + 面 (Side).
- 白面 Wheat flour: 白 (White) + 面 (Flour).

166. 立 (Lì) Stand, erect, vertical, lift, immediate.

Note: Pictogram of a **vertically erected** mound.
- 立法 Legislation: 立 (Erect) + 法 (Law).
- 立马 Immediately: 立 (Immediate) + 马 (Horse).
- 对立 Face, oppose: 对 (Opposite) + 立 (Stand).

167. 着 (Zhe) Suffix indicating continuous action. (Zháo) Touch, contact, suffix that indicates the result of the action (zhuó) Dress, come into contact with.

Note: Associative character of a person observing (看) his sheep (羊) **continuously**. See character no. 106 and 159.
- 走着 Be walking: 走 (Walk) + 着 (Continuous action).
- 着火 Catch fire, be on fire: 着 (Suffix result of the action) + 火 (Fire).

168. 行 (Xíng) Walk, travel, doing, behavior, conduct. (háng) Row, line, industry, business.

Note: Pictogram of a **crossroads**. When it is part of another character, its simplified writing is 彳.
- 出行 Travel, leave: 出 (Exit) + 行 (Travel).
- 行人 Pedestrian: 行 (Walk) + 人 (Person).

169. 气 (Qì) Gas, air, climate, atmosphere, smell, spirit, Anger.

Note: Pictogram of **vapors** rising.
- 天气 Climate: 天 (Sky) + 气 (Atmosphere).
- 生气 Get angry: 生 (Born) + 气 (Anger).
- 气体 Gas: 气 (Air) + 体 (Body).

170. 肉 (Ròu) Meat, flesh.

Note: Pictogram of the internal part of a person (人). When it is part of another character, its writing is simplifed as 月, ideogram of ribs. See character no. 1 and 8.
- 牛肉 Beef: 牛 (Cow) + 肉 (Meat).
- 羊肉 Lamb meat: 羊 (Sheep) + 肉 (Meat).

171. 卜 (Bǔ) Divine, tell fortunes, foretell, predicy. (Bo) Radish.

Note: Indicative character of a crack in the shell of a turtle, an artifact used in ancient times for **divination**.

172. 占 (Zhān) Practise divination. (Zhàn) Occupy, Take, possess, seize.

Note: Associative character of a mouth (口) **practicing divination** (卜). See character no. 2 and 171.
- 占地 Occupy a territory: 占 (Occupy) + 地 (Land).
- 占卜 Fortune telling: 占 (Practise divination) + 卜 (Predicy).

173. 付 (Fù) Pay, deliver, give.

Note: Associative character of a person (人=亻) **paying** for an inch (寸) of some commodity. See character no. 1 and 65.
- 现付 Pay in cash: 现 (Present) + 付 (Pay).

174. 千 (Qiān) Thousand, a lot.

Note: Indicative character for a thousand units of something, an amount immensely greater than ten (十) by adding one more stroke at the top. See character no. 100.
- 一千 Thousand: 一 (One) + 千 (Thousand).
- 三千 Three Thousand: 三 (Three) + 千 (Thousand).
- 上千 More than One Thousand: 上 (Up) + 千 (Thousand).

175. 种 (Zhǒng) Type, class, race, species. (zhòng) Plant, cultivate.

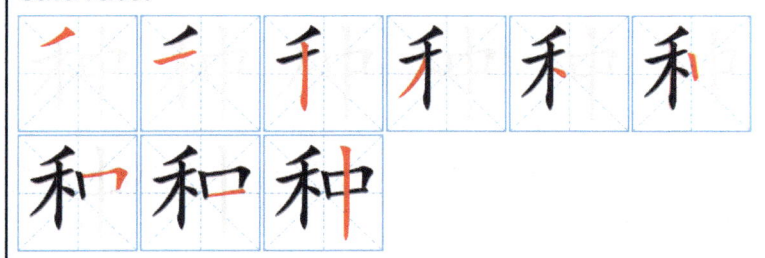

Note: Picto-phonetic character of a grain type (禾) and center (中), the left side (禾) give a semantic connotation of a grain **class**. The right side (中 = zhōng) a phonetic, in order to help remember its pronunciation. See character no. 40 and 158.
- 种子 Seed: 种 (Plant) + 子 (Son).
- 人种 Race (of a person): 人 (Person) + 种 (Class).

176. 叫 (Jiào) Call, shout, order, ask.

Note: Indicative character of a hook (丩) coming out of a mouth (口) exemplifying **calling** someone by name. See character no. 2.
- 大叫 Shout: 大 (Big) + 叫 (Call).
- 叫车 call a taxi: 叫 (Call) + 车 (Car).

177. 犬 (Quǎn) Dog.

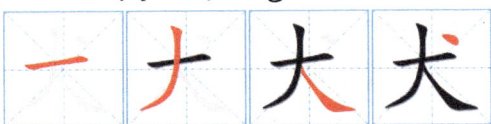

Note: Pictogram of a large **dog** (大) with its tongue out. When it is part of another character, its simplified writing is 犭. See character no. 5.

The Logic of Chinese Characters

178. 打 (Dǎ) Hit, strike, knock, fight

Note: Associative character of a hand (手 = 扌) hammering **(hitting)** a nail (丁). See character no. 15 and 164.
- 打字 Type: 打 (Hit) + 字 (Character).
- 打车 Take a taxi: 打 (Take) + 车 (Car).
- 打中 Hit the target: 打 (Hit) + 中 (Center).

179. 止 (Zhǐ) Finish, stop, stay.

Note: Character indicative of a foot (足) in a vertical position with the heel down and the toes on top, indicating the state of **stopping**. See character no. 54.
- 中止 Interrupt, discontinue: 中 (Center) + 止 (Stop).

180. 舌 (Shé) Tongue.

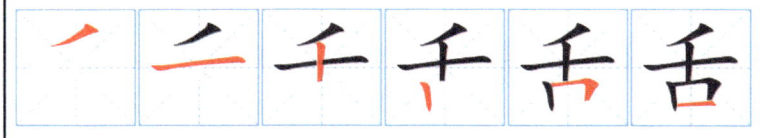

Note: Associative character of a mouth (口) releasing a thousand (千) words through the use of the tongue. See character no. 2 and 174.
- 舌头 Tongue: 舌 (Tongue) + 头 (Head).

181. 尤 (Yóu) Particular, exceptional, extraordinary, defect.

Note: Character indicative of a dog (犬) limping on one foot, a defect that made it **particular**. See character no. 77.
- 尤为 Especially: 尤 (Exceptional) + 为 (Act).

182. 京 (Jīng) Capital, abbreviation of Beijing province.

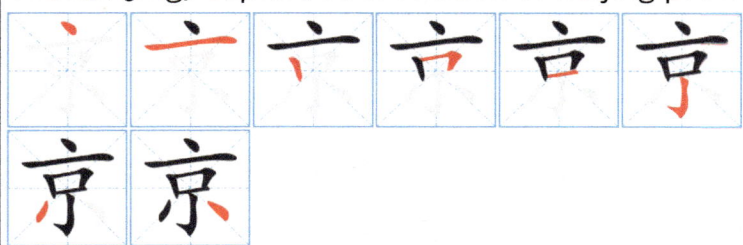

Note: Associative character of a building with a small (小) entrance (口) under its roof illustrating the central buildings of the capital of a country. See character no. 2 and 35.

183. 军 (Jūn) Army, armed force, military.

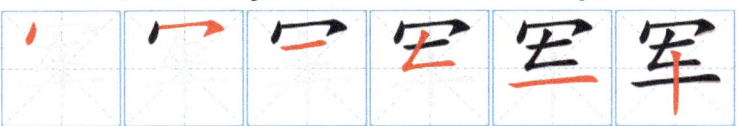

Note: Indicative character of a covered (冖) or armored carriage (车) for war. See character no. 140.
- 军人 Soldier: 军 (Military) + 人 (Person).
- 军区 Militarized zone: 军 (Military) + 区 (Zone).
- 军长 Army Commander: 军 (Army) + 区 (Elder).

184. 兄 (Xiōng) Older brother, older man.

Note: Associative character of a son (儿) taking the floor to speak (口) as a right that the eldest son received. See character no. 2 and 60.

185. 样 (Yàng) Model, type, pattern, class, appearance.

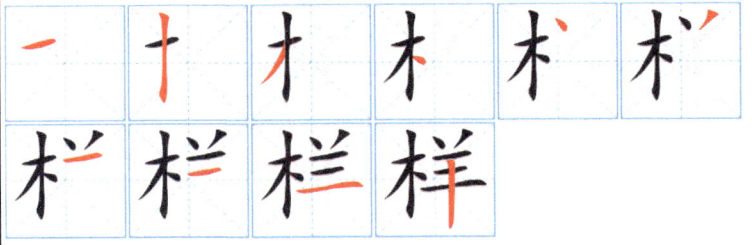

Note: Picto-phonetic character of a sheep (羊) eating a specific **kind of** vegetation, represented by a tree (木). The character on the right (羊=Yáng) also serves a phonetic function as a reminder of its pronunciation. See character no. 9 and 159.
- 一样 Same, equal: 一 (One) + 样 (Type).
- 样子 Appearance: 样 (Appearance) + 子 (Diminutive suffix for objects).

186. 旦 (Dàn) Dawn, sunrise, morning.

Note: Indicative character of the sun (日) rising above the earth, exemplifying **dawn**. See character no. 2.
- 一旦 In a single day: 一 (One) + 旦 (Dawn).

187. 思 (Sī) Think, consider, yearn.

<u>Note:</u> Associative character of the heart (心) of someone **thinking** about their field (田). See character no. 21 and 28.
- 思想 Thought, idea: 思 (Consider) + 想 (Think).

188. 灭 (Miè) Go out (light, fire etc.)Extinguish, exterminate, destroy.

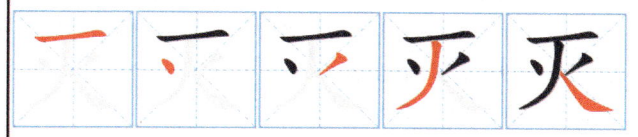

<u>Note:</u> Indicative character of a fire (火) being **extinguished**. See character no. 11.
- 灭火 Put out a fire: 灭 (Extinguish) + 火 (Fire).

189. 得 (De) Get, obtain, gain. (Děi) Most, have to.

<u>Note:</u> Indicative character of a person going for a walk (行=彳) at dawn (旦) to harvest his portion (寸) of land, here represented by an inch, in order to **obtain** his profit. See character no. 65, 168 and 186.
- 得到 Get, obtain: 得 (Get) + 到 (Until).
- 得分 Score, get a point: 得 (Get) + 分 (Point).

190. 正 (De) Correct, right, straighten, main, positive.

<u>Note:</u> Indicative character of a foot (足) walking a single **straight** path (一). See character no. 54 and 179.
- 公正 Justice, impartial: 公 (Public) + 正 (Right).
- 立正 Stand up straight: 立 (stand) + 正 (Straight).

191. 古 (Gǔ) Ancient, age-old.

<u>Note:</u> Associative character of ten (十) mouths (口) exemplifying ancient traditions that were transmitted verbally, that is, by word of mouth. See character no. 2 and 100.
- 古时 Antiquity: 古 (age-old) + 时 (Time).
- 古文 Ancient writings: 古 (Ancient) + 文 (Writing).

192. 性 (xìng) Sex, character, quality, gender, disposition, nature.

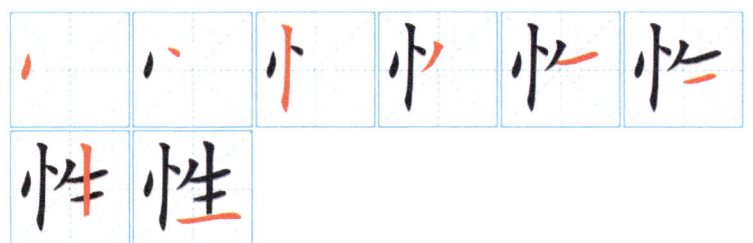

<u>Note:</u> Picto-phonetic character about the **nature or character**, represented by a heart (心 = 忄) of a person from birth (生). The character on the left (心 =Xīn) also serves a phonetic function as a reminder of its pronunciation. See character no. 28 and 51.
- 天性 Natural instinct: 天 (Sky) + 性 (Nature).
- 同性 Same-sex: 同 (Same) + 性 (Gender).
- 男性 Masculine gender: 男 (Male) + 性 (Gender).

193. 就 (Jiù) So, immediately after, in relation to, precisely.

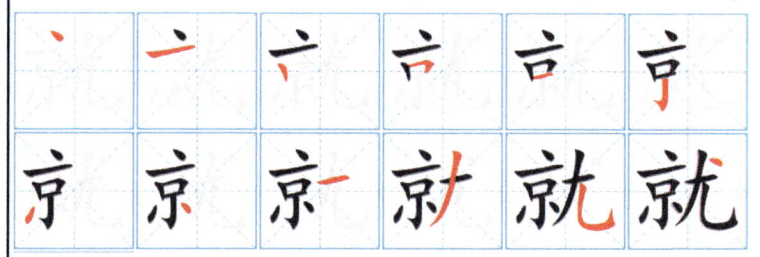

Note: Associative character of how special (尤) the central building of the capital (京) is **in relation to** others. See character no. 181 and 182.
- 成就 Achievement, success: 成 (Succeed) + 就 (In relation to).

194. 其 (Qí) This, his, his, he, she, it, other, another.

Note: Pictogram of a raised column with two stones indicating that this territory belonged to **another person, his or hers.**
- 其他 Other: 其 (Other) + 他 (He).

195. 那 (Nà) That, so, then, in that case.

Note: Character indicative of a mountainous region (阝) where people with very long hair lived, considered **as those** people who were not part of the town. See character no. 53.
- 那里 There, there, there: 那 (That) + 里 (Inside).
- 那个 That, that, that: 那 (That) + 个 (measurement word).
- 那样 That type, like this, that way: 那 (That) + 样 (Form).

196. 北 (Běi) North.

<u>Note:</u> Pictogram of two soldiers standing back to back guarding the **north** of the city.
- 北京 Beijing: 北 (North) + 京 (City).
- 北方 Northern part: 北 (North) + 方 (Place).

197. 东 (Dōng) East, orient, host.

<u>Note:</u> Indicative character of a carriage (车) moving to the **east** of the country. See character no. 140.
- 中东 Middle East: 中 (Center) + 东 (East).
- 东北 Northeast: 东 (East) + 北 (North).

198. 南 (Nán) South, southern.

<u>Note:</u> Indicative character of a door (门) that faces the **southern** territory (土) of the country where sheep were raised (羊). See character no. 4, 17 and 159.
- 南面 Southern side: 南 (South) + 面 (Side).

199. 西 (Xī) West.

Note: Borrowed character due to its pronunciation and pictogram similar to the number four (四=Sì)
- 东西 Thing, object: 东 (East) + 西 (West).

200. 边 (Biān) Edge, side, border, margin.

Note: Associative character of walking (走=辶) with a tool (力) in order to defend the **borders**. See character no. 12 and 61.
- 里边 Inner side: 里 (Inside) + 边 (Side).
- 边区 Border zone: 边 (Border) + 区 (Zone).

201. 它 (Tā) It, this, that (for things).

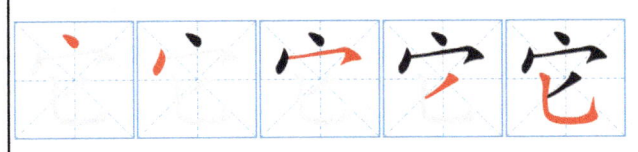

Note: Pictogram of a spoon (匕) in a house (宀) incicating the way to call objects: **It, that, this**.
- 它们 Those, those (third person plural for things): 它 (It) + 们 (Plural suffix).

202. 要 (Yào) Want, desire, have to, go to do (something).

Note: Associative character of a woman (女) **wanting** to go west (西). See character no. 10 and 199.
- 要去 Want to go: 要 (Want) + 去 (Go).

203. 比 (Bǐ) Compare, compete, contrast, copy.

Note: Pictogram of two spoons (匕) placed side by side and **compared**. See character no. 201.
- 比如 For example: 比 (Compare) + 如 (If conditional).
- 可比 Comparable: 可 (Power) + 比 (Compare).
- 比对 Check by comparing: 比 (Compare) + 对 (Correct).

204. 兑 (Duì) Exchange, change, convert, add.

Note: Indicative character of the older brother (兄) **exchanging** Goods, represented by the number eight (八). See character no. 98 and 184.
- 兑现 Cash (a check): 兑 (Exchange) + 现 (Present).

205. 能 (Néng) Power, skill, capacity, ability, technique, energy.

Note: Pictogram of a bear rotated at 90 degrees. The simplified character for meat (肉 = 月) is used to represent the body, 厶 represents the mouth giving a howl, and 匕 the legs. The bear is a symbol of **power** and **energy**.
- 全能 Almighty: 全 (Complete) + 能 (Power).
- 体能 Physical ability: 体 (Body) + 能 (Ability).

206. 夕 (Xī) Sunset, dusk, night.

Note: Pictogram of a part of the moon (月) appearing at **sunset**. Also like 月 is the simplified character for meat. See character no. 8 and 170.

207. 话 (Huà) Word, speak, talk.

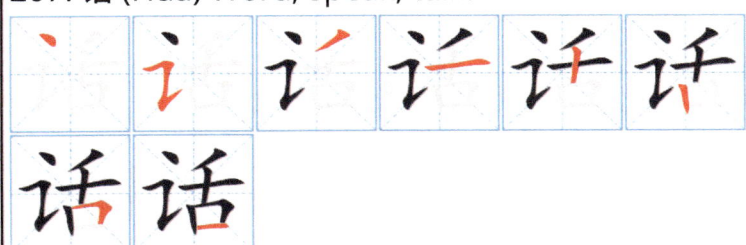

Note: Associative character of a tongue (舌) **speaking words** (言 =讠). See character no. 133 and 180.
- 电话 Telephone: 电 (Electricity) + 话 (Word).
- 土话 Dialect of a place, slang: 土 (Land) + 话 (Word).
- 对话 Have a conversation, dialogue: 对 (Reply) + 话 (Speak).

208. 家 (Jiā) Family, house, home, expert.

Note: Indicative character of a pig (豕) in a house, represented by a roof (宀) indicating that it was not a wild pig, but rather belonged to a **family**.
- 国家 Country: 国 (Nation) + 家 (Family).
- 成家 Get married, start a family: 成 (establish) + 家 (Family).
- 家人 Family, family member: 家 (Family) + 人 (Person).

209. 买 (Mǎi) Buy, purchase.

Note: Indicative character of a person with an empty basket on his head going **shopping**. See character no. 56.
- 买家 Buyer: 买 (Buy) + 家 (Expert).

210. 卖 (Mài) Sell.

Note: Indicative character of a person with a basket on his head full of things going to **sell** them. See character no. 56 and 209.
- 买卖 Buying and selling: 买 (Buy) + 卖 (Sell).
- 卖肉 Sell meat: 卖 (Sell) + 肉 (Meat).

211. 多 (Duō) Much, more, many, excessive, how.

<u>Note:</u> Indicative character of two pieces of meat (肉 = 夕), something that could represent **a lot of** meat. See character no. 170 and 206.
- 多大 How old?: 多 (How) + 大 (Big).
- 多少 how many: 多 (Many) + 少 (Little).

212. 说 (Shuō) Say, speak, explain.

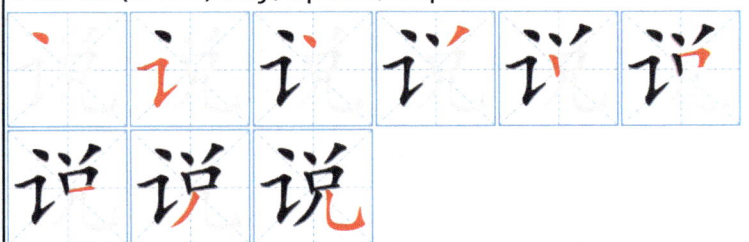

<u>Note:</u> Associative character of a **conversation, talking** and exchanging (兑) words (言 = 讠). See character no. 133 and 204.
- 说话 Speak, talk: 说 (Say) + 话 (Word).
- 说法 Way of speaking: 说 (Speak) + 法 (Manner).

213. 尔 (Ěr) You, this one, that one. (old Chinese, no longer used alone).

<u>Note:</u> Indicative character of a small (小) sprout about to be born, the origin of everything, a scene that exemplifies the idea of "**You**". See character no. 35.

214. 你 (Nǐ) You.

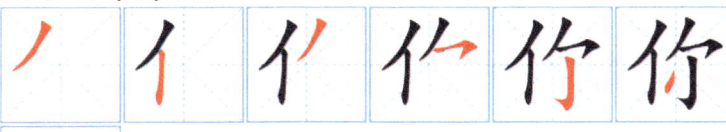

Note: Associative character of person (人 = 亻) and "You" in ancient Chinese (尔) in order to form the concept of "**You**" in modern Chinese. See character no. 1 and 213.
- 你好 Hello!: 你 (You) + 好 (Good).

215. 作 (Zuò) Do, produce, compose, be considered as.

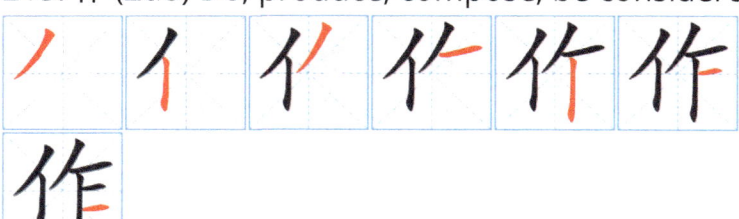

Note: Associative character of a person (人=亻) weaving (乍) **producing** clothes. See character no. 1.
- 工作 Work: 工 (Work) + 作 (Do).
- 作家 Writer: 作 (Compose) + 家 (Expert).

216. 者 (Zhě) Suffix of person, personification.

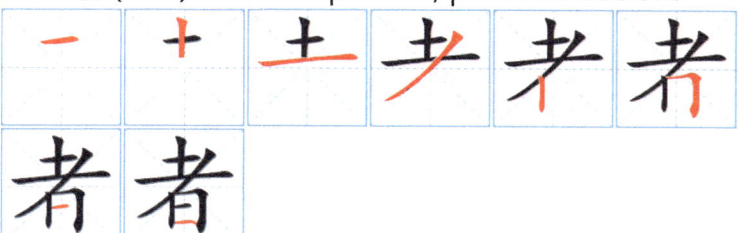

Note: Indicative character that represents the connection and **personification** of elements such as the sun (日) or the earth (土). See character no. 3 and 4.
- 作者 Author: 作 (Produce) + 者 (Suffix of person).
- 听者 Listener: 听 (Hear) + 者 (Person suffix).

217. 丝 (Sī) Silk.

Note: Pictogram of two strands of **silk** (纟) making a thread (一). When it is part of another character, its writing is simplified as 纟.
- 肉丝 shredded meat: 肉 (Meat) + 丝 Silk).

218. 外 (Wài) Exterior, external, outside, foreign, foreigner.

Note: Associative character that conveys the idea of predicting the future (卜) what will happen **outside** watching the sunset (夕). See character no. 170 and 206.
- 国外 Foreign country: 国 (Country) + 外 (Foreign).
- 外人 Stranger, stranger: 外 (Foreign) + 国 (Person).
- 外用 For external use: 外 (External) + 用 (Use).

219. 名 (Míng) Name, fame.

Note: Associative character of a mouth (口) pronouncing someone's **name** at dusk (夕), in order to locate it. See character no. 2 and 206.
- 有名 Famous: 有 (Have) + 名 (Fame).
- 名字 Name: 名 (Name) + 字 (Letter).
- 名言 Famous saying: 名 (Famous) + 言 (Word).

220. 户 (Hù) Door, family, home, bank account.

Note: Pictogram of a single-leaf door, typical of a Chinese **home** in ancient times.
- 户外 Outdoor: 户 (Door) + 外 (Outside).
- 户口 Household registration: 户 (Household) + 口 (measurement word for family member).
- 开户 Open a bank account: 开 (Open) + 户 (Bank account).

221. 点 (Diǎn) Drop, stain, spots, a little, mark, review, turn on.

Note: Associative character of divination (占) by the light of fire (火 = 灬), using certain **marks** or **spots** on the skin of some animal. See character no. 11 and 172.
- 一点 A little: 一 (one) + 点 (A little).
- 几点 What time is it?: 几 (How many) + 点 (Points).
- 七点 Seven o'clock: 七 (Seven) + 点 (Points).
- 观点 Point of view: 观 (View) + 点 (Point).

222. 当 (Dāng) Equal, equivalent, duty, proper, appropriate, work as, be, act as.

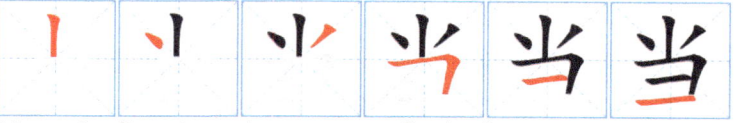

Note: Indicative character of a balance weighing two elements with an **equivalent** weight.
- 当日 This same day: 当 (Equal) + 日 (Day).
- 想当 Want to be, want to become: 想 (Want) + 当 (Be).
- 当作 Consider as: 当 (Act as) + 作 (Be considered as).

223. 信 (Xìn) Letter, message, believe.

Note: Associative character of a person (人 = 亻) delivering a **message** verbally (言), which made it totally **credible**. See character no. 1 and 133.
- 相信 Believe: 相 (Appearance) + 信 (Believe).
- 信心 Faith, trust: 信 (Believe) + 心 (Heart).
- 口信 Verbal message: 口 (Mouth) + 信 (Message).

224. 市 (Shì) Market, city, business.

Note: Indicative character of a door (门) with a roof or awning (宀) which represents a **business** and not a private house. See character no. 17.
- 上市 Launch on the market, go on sale: 上 (Up) + 市 (Market).
- 市长 City Mayor: 市 (City) + 长 (Old).

225. 都 (Dōu) All, both, entirely. (Dū) Capital, metropolis.

Note: Indicative character of a city (阝) with **all** the inhabitants (者) in it. See character no. 53 and 216.
- 古都 Old Capital: 古 (Old) + 都 (Capital).
- 大都 In general, for the most part: 大 (Big) + 都 (All).

226. 经 (Jīng) Go through, pass through, writings, manage, menstruation.

Note: Associative character that describes the manual work (工) of the silk (丝 = 纟) **passing** continuously through the loom. See character no. 18, 77 and 217.
- 经理 Manager: 经 (Manage) + 理 (Administrate).
- 月经 Menstruation: 月 (Month) + 经 (Menstruation).
- 经文 Verse (of a sacred writing): 经 (Writings) + 文 (Text).

227. 起 (Qǐ) Start, begin, get up, rise.

Note: Extended meaning character of **getting up** and already (已) having left (走). See character no. 61 and 137.
- 起立 Stand up: 起 (Get up) + 立 (stand).
- 想起 Remember, bring to mind: 想 (Think) + 起 (begin).

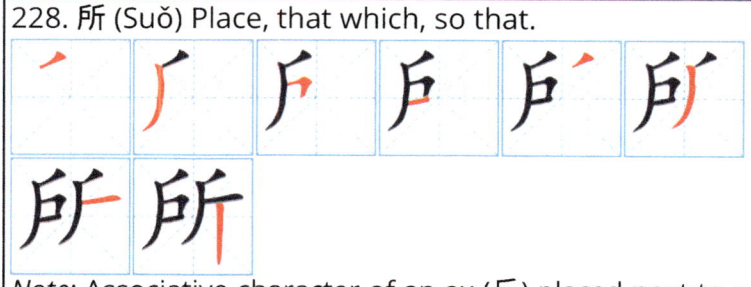

228. 所 (Suǒ) Place, that which, so that.

Note: Associative character of an ax (斤) placed next to a door (户), the **place** where it used to be placed. See character no. 102 and 220.
- 所以 Therefore: 所 (So that) + 以 (By means of).

229. 活 (Huó) Live, life, save, alive.

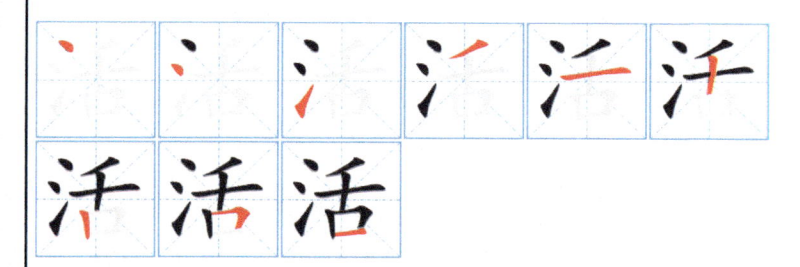

Note: Associative character of a tongue (舌) drinking water (水 = 氵), the vital liquid for **life**. See character no. 7 and ´80.
- 生活 Life, live: 生 (Life) + 活 (Live).
- 活动 Train, exercise: 活 (Live) + 动 (Move).

230. 然 (Rán) So, that way, like that, right, correct.

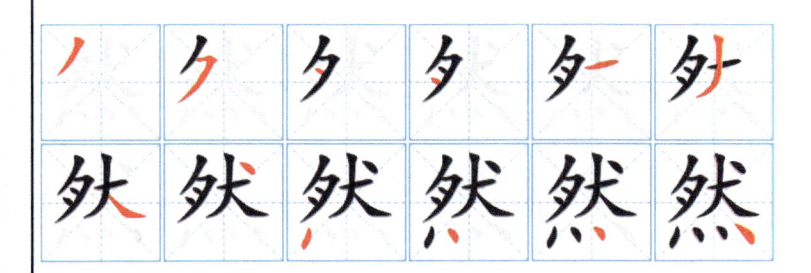

Note: Associative character of meat (肉=月) of dog (犬) placed on the fire (火 = 灬) to make a sacrifice, exemplifying the **correct** way to make sacrifices. See character no. 11, 170 and 177.
- 自然 Nature: 自 (Oneself) + 然 (So).
- 果然 As expected: 果 (Result) + 然 (Like that).

231. 事 (Rán) Thing, subject, matter, work.

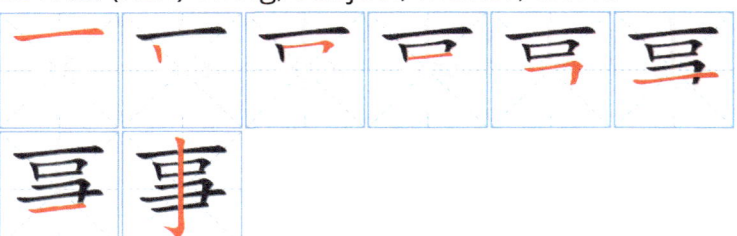

Note: Pictogram of a hand (手 = 扌) holding a prey that it has hunted and pierced through the mouth (口) with a spear, obtaining **something** to eat. See character no. 2 and 15.
- 有事 Be busy: 有 (Have) + 事 (Work).
- 同事 Coworker: 同 (Same) + 事 (Subject).
- 实事 Real event: 实 (Real) + 事 (Matter).

232. 早 (Zǎo) In the morning, morning, early, in advance.

Note: Indicative character of the sun (日) at its maximum, represented by the number ten (十), exemplifying **morning**. See character no. 3 and 100.
- 早起 Get up early: 早 (Morning) + 起 (Get up).
- 早上好 Good morning!: 早 (Morning) + 上 (Up) + 好 (Good).

233. 台 (Tái) Platform, terrace, stage, counter, station.

Note: Pictogram of a platform for making sacrifices.
- 上台 Go on stage: 上 (Up) + 台 (Stage).
- 电台 Broadcaster, TV station: 电 (Electricity) + 台 (Station).

234. 汉 (Hàn) Chinese Han ethnic group, Han ethnic man, Chinese people, China.

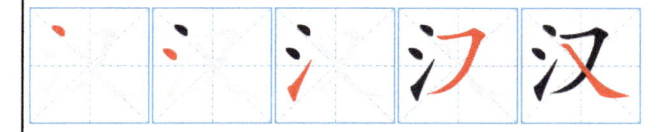

Note: Associative character of a person represented by a right hand (又) next to the yellow river (水=氵), the place where the **Chinese people** supposedly originated. See character no. 7 and 77.
- 汉字 Chinese characters: 汉 (Chinese) + 字 (Character).
- 好汉 Brave man: 好 (Good) + 汉 (Han ethnic man).

235. 前 (Qián) In front, in front of, forward, previous, first, before.

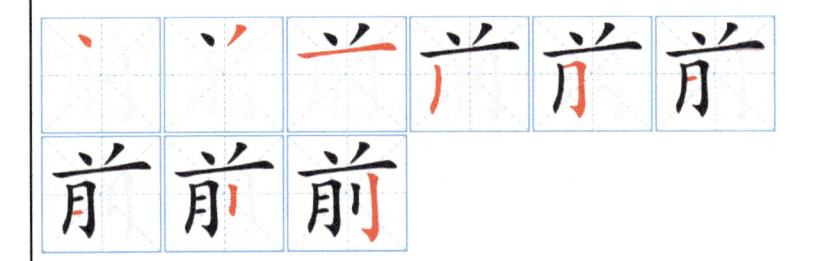

Note: Indicative character of a knife (刀+ 刂) **in front of** a piece of meat to cut it (肉=月). See character no. 69 and 170.
- 目前 In the present, now: 目 (Eye) + 前 (In front of).
- 事前 In advance, before the event: 事 (Subject) + 前 (Previous).

236. 美 (Měi) Beautiful, prettify

Note: Associative character of a fat (大) sheep (羊), something that was considered beautiful for its value. See character no. 5 and 159.
- 美国 United States: 美 (Beautiful) + 国 (Country).
- 美女 Beautiful woman: 美 (Pretty) + 女 (Woman).

237. 首 (Shǒu) Head, leader. First.

Note: Pictogram of a **head** where the nose (自), the forehead and two hairs stand out. See character no. 101.
- 首付 Initial payment: 首 (First) + 付 (Payment).

238. 业 (Yè) Business, trade, industry, ocupation, job, profession, Company.

Note: Pictogram of a structure where musical instruments for sale were hung, representing the music **industry**.
- 工业 Industry: 工 (Work) + 业 (Industry).
- 开业 Start a business: 开 (Open) + 业 (Company).
- 业主 Business owner: 业 (business) + 主 (Owner).

239. 但 (Dàn) But, yet, still, however, only, merely.

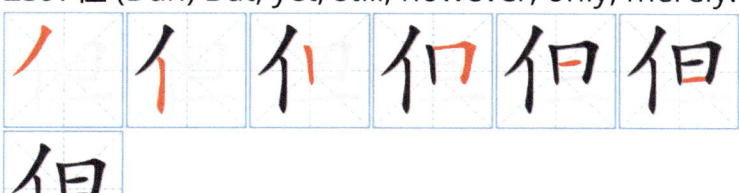

Note: Associative character of a person (人+亻) in the dawn (旦) **only** for the purpose of work. See character no. 1 and 186.
- 但是 But: 但 (But) + 是 (Be).
- 不但 Not only: 不 (No) + 但 (Only).

240. 高 (Gāo) High, tall.

Note: Pictogram of a tall multi-story building, with the first floor (同), the second floor (口) and the roof (亠).
- Expert 高手: 高 (High) + 手 (Hand).
- 高明 Intelligent: 高 (High) + 明 (Bright).

241. 计 (Jì) Count, plan, stratagem, number, calculate.

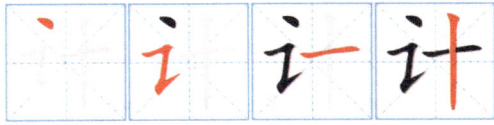

Note: Indicative character of a person **counting** out loud (言 + 讠) to the number ten (十). See character no. 100 and 133.
- 生计 Livelihood, sustenance: 生 (Life) + 计 (Count).
- 计时 Count time: 计 (Count) + 时 (Time).

242. 与 (Yǔ) Give, offer, assist, and. (yù) participate.

Note: Pictogram of a shortcut that connects two roads, in order to **assist** pedestrians.
- 与会 Participate in a meeting: 与 (Participate) + 会 (Meeting).

243. 井 (Jǐng) Well, hole, clean, tidy, orderly.

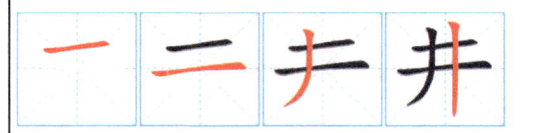

Note: Pictogram of the **ordered** location of the **wells** in the land cultivation system in ancient times, where the well was located in the center surrounded by eight plots.

244. 产 (Chǎn) Produce, give birth, product, property.

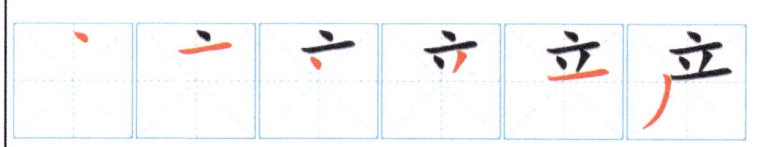

Note: Indicative character of a mound (立) on top of a factory (厂) indicating that it is in full **production**. See character no. 130 and 166.
- 生产 Produce: 生 (Born) + 产 (Produce).
- 产业 Producing industry: 产 (Produce) + 业 (Industry).

245. 老 (Lǎo) Old, elder, outdated, frequent, always.

Note: Associative character of a piece of land (土) that is more than seventy (七) years **old**, indicating something very old. See character no. 4 and 97.
- 年老 Old man: 年 (Year) + 老 (Old).
- 老手 Veteran, experienced: 老 (Old) + 手 (Hand).

246. 位 (Wèi) Position, place, measurement word for people.

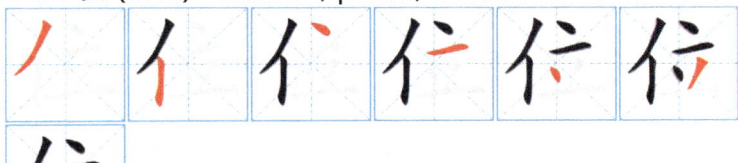

Note: Associative character of a person (人) standing up (立) to take his position. See character no. 1 and 166.
- 车位 Parking: 车 (Vehicle) + 位 (Position).
- 学位 Academic degree, title: 学 (Study) + 位 (Position).
- 定位 Locator, position of something: 定 (Stable) + 位 (Position).

247. 此 (Cǐ) This one, that, here.

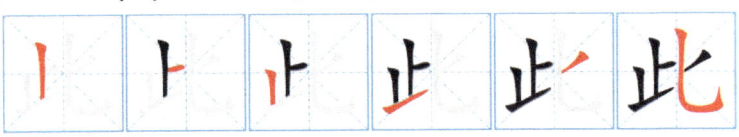

Note: Indicative character of a foot (足) approaching a spoon (匕), which is **this** person's. See character no. 54 and 201.
- 对此 Regarding: 对 (Opposite) + 此 (This).
- 从此 From now on, since then: 从 (Since) + 此 (Here).

248. 两 (Liǎng) Two, both, a couple of.

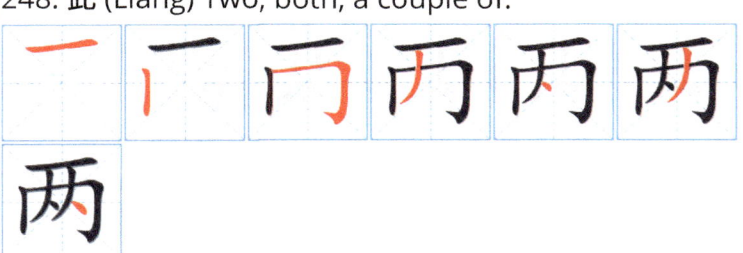

<u>Note:</u> Pictogram of **two** people (人) entering through a door (门). See character no. 1 and 17.
- 两面 Both sides: 两 (Two) + 面 (Side).
- 两位 Two people: 两 (Two) + 位 (Measurement word for people).

249. 无 (Wú) No, nothing, no have, without.

<u>Note:</u> Pictogram of a person dancing in a ritual during the time of drought when there **was no** water.
- 无力 Lack of strength: 无 (No) + 力 (Strength).
- 无用 Useless: 无 (Not) + 用 (Useful).
- 无言 Not having anything to say: 无 (No) + 言 (Word).

250. 政 (Zhèng) Politics, government.

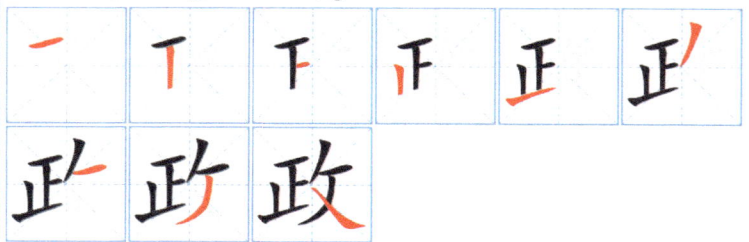

<u>Note:</u> Picto-phonetic character of a hand (又) ordering to do the right thing (正), the work of government. The left side 正 =Zhèng gives a phonetic connotation, in order to help remember its pronunciation. See character no. 77 and 190.
- 政体 Government: 政 (Government) + 体 (Body).
- 行政 Administration: 行 (Business) + 政 (Government).
- 国内政 Internal policy of a country: 国 (Country) + 内 (Interior) + 政 (Politics).

251. 道 (Dào) Way, path, road, channel, doctrine, principle.

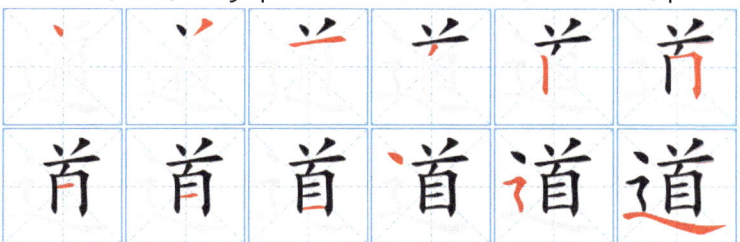

Note: Associative character of a person's thoughts, represented by their head (首) following a **path** (走=辶). See character no. 61 and 237.
- 正道 The right path, the true doctrine: 正 (Correct) + 道 (Doctrine).
- 车道 Traffic lane: 车 (Vehicle) + 道 (Road).
- 水道 Aqueduct: 水 (Water) + 道 (Road).

252. Change, transform, digest, dissolve, -ize, -ify (suffix).

Note: Pictogram of two people (人=亻), one standing and the other upside down (匕) representing change. See character no. 1
- 文化 Culture: 文 (Writing) + 化 (Transform).
- 化学 chemistry: 化 (Transform) + 学 (Study).
- 美化 Beautify: 美 (Beauty) + 化 (Transform).

253. 进 (Jìn) Advance, enter, move forward, receive, take.

Note: Picto-phonetic character of a person **advancing on the way** (走=辶) to the well (井). The right side 井 =Jǐng gives a phonetic connotation, in order to help remember its pronunciation. See character no. 61 and 243.
- 进来 Enter: 进 (Enter) + 来 (Come).
- 进口 Import: 进 (Enter) + 口 (Entry).
- 进化 Evolution: 进 (Advance) + 化 (Transform).

254. 部 (Bù) Part, unit, troops, section, office.

Note: Associative character of the people (口) of a city (里=阝) standing (立) representing the government **office**. See character no. 2, 53 and 166.
- 部分 Part, piece of something: 部 (Part) + 分 (Separate).
- 部长 Department head: 部 (Office) + 长 (Old).

255. 支 (Zhī) Put, hold, endure, send, pay.

Note: Associative character of a hand (又) holding some soil (土). See character no. 4 and 77.
- 支付 Pay: 支 (Pay) + 付 (Pay).
- 开支 Expenses, expenses: 开 (Open) + 支 (Pay).

256. 队 (Duì) Group, team, row.

Note: Indicative character of a **group** of people (人) walking in a row on a mountain (里=阝) in order not to fall. See character no. 1 and 53.
- 军队 Army troops: 军 (Army) + 队 (Equipment).
- 队友 Teammate: 队 (Team) + 友 (Friend).

257. 些 (Xiē) Some, a few.

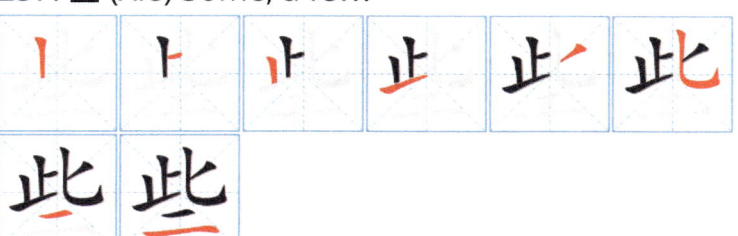

Note: Indicative character of this (此) plus two (二) are three, that is, "**some**." See character no. 92 and 247.
- 一些 Some: 一 (One) + 些 (Some).
- 这些 These: 这 (This) + 些 (Some).

258. 耳 (Ěr) Ear.

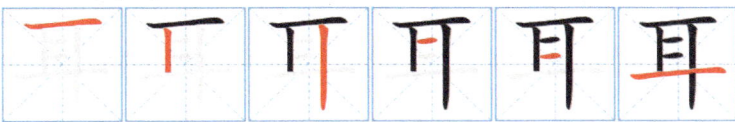

Note: Pictogram of an **ear**.
- 耳机 Headphones: 耳 (Ear) + 机 (Machine).

259. 取 (Qǔ) Take, get, hold, choose, assume.

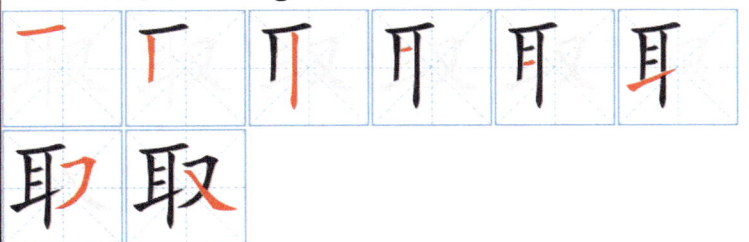

Note: Character with extended sense of a hand (又) **holding** an ear (耳), something that was common in wars. Soldiers who cut off their enemies' ears in battle were rewarded. See character no. 77 and 258.
- 取得 Achieve, obtain: 取 (Obtain) + 得 (Obtain).
- 取回 Retrieve: 取 (Get) + 回 (Return).

260. 功 (Gōng) Merit, achievement, ability, effect, result.

Note: Associative nature of applying force (力) to work (工) produces **results**. See character no. 12 and 18.
- 取得 Achieve, obtain: 取 (Obtain) + 得 (Obtain).
- 成功 Success: 成 (Succeed) + 功 (Achievement).
- 功能 Function: 功 (Result) + 能 (ability).

261. 米 (Mǐ) Rice, meter.

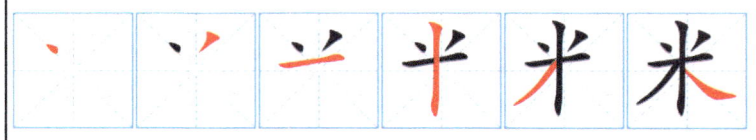

Note: Pictogram of two grains of **rice** hanging from the plant (木). See character no. 9.
- 千米 Kilometer: 千 (Thousand) + 米 (Meter).
- 玉米 Corn: 玉 (Jade) + 米 (Rice).
- 生米 Raw rice: 生 (Raw) + 米 (Rice).

262. 音 (Yīn) Sound, tone, news.

Note: Character with extended meaning of a person standing (立) in front of the sun (日), paying homage to it by emitting singing **sounds**. See character no. 3 and 166.
- 发音 Pronunciation: 发 (Emit) + 音 (Sound).
- 元音 Vowel: 元 (Main) + 音 (Sound).
- 口音 Accent: 口 (Mouth) + 音 (Tone).

263. 很 (Hěn) Very, very much, many.

Note: Character with extended meaning of a person walking (行=彳) on **many** roads (艮) under the sun (日). See character no. 168.
- 很多 Many: 很 (Very) + 多 (Much).
- 很大 Very big: 很 (Very) + 大 (Big).

264. 华 (Huá) Magnificent, prosperous, China.

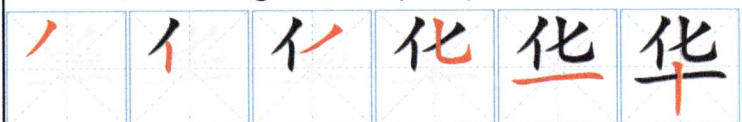

Note: Associative character of "change" (化) until **perfection** (十) or **optimality** is reached. See character no. 100 and 252.
- 华人 Person of Chinese origin: 华 (China) + 人 (Person).
- 华美 Magnificent, splendid: 华 (Magnificent) + 美 (Beautiful).

265. 示 (Shì) Show, indicate, notify.

Note: Pictogram of a small (小) altar showing a sacrifice. When it is part of another character, its writing is simplified as 礻.
- 出示 Show: 出 (Exit) + 示 (Show).

266. 矢 (Shǐ) Arrow.

Note: Pictogram of an **arrow** crossing the sky (天). See character no. 29.

267. 书 (Shū) Book, document, letter, calligraphy.

Note: Pictogram of a hand (手 = 扌) writing on a **book**. See character no. 15.
- 看书 Read a book: 看 (Watch) + 书 (Book).
- 一本书 One book: 一 (One) + 本 (Measurement word) + 书 (Book).

268. 并 (Bìng) Simultaneously, equally, combine, mix, and.

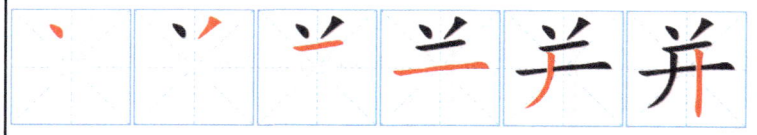

Note: Pictogram of the two leaves of a door opening (开) simultaneously. See character no. 19.
- 并发 Complication: 并 (Simultaneously) + 发 (Send).

269. 巴 (Bā) Wait, character used for transliterations.

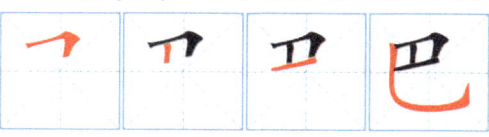

Note: Pictogram of a snake with its mouth open eagerly waiting to eat its prey.
- 巴西 Brazil: 巴 (Transliteration) + 西 (West).
- 古巴 Cuba: 古 (Old) + 巴 (Transliteration).

270. 才 (Cái) Skill, talent, gift, ability, just.

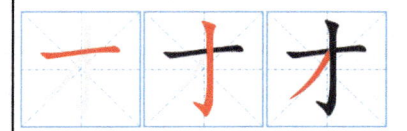

<u>Note:</u> Pictogram of a person (大) jumping showing his **skills**. See character no. 5.
- 人才 Talented person: 人 (Person) + 才 (Talent).
- 口才 Eloquence: 口 (Mouth) + 才 (Talent).
- 天才 Innate Talent: 天 (Sky) + 才 (Talent).

271. 最 (Zuì) Most, the better, -est (superlative degree).

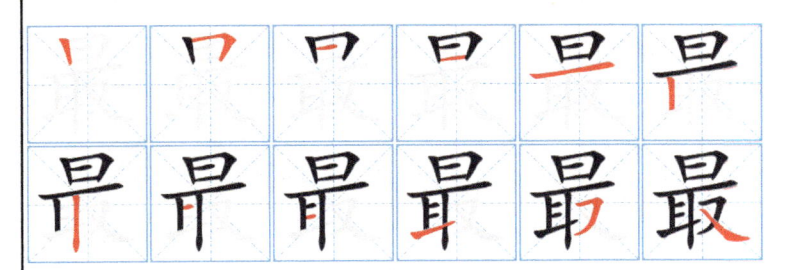

Note: Associative character of someone taking (取) "the best", represented by the sun (日). See character no. 3 and 259.
- 最高 The highest: 最 (Most) + 高 (High).
- 最后 The last thing, finally: 最 (-est superlative degree) + 后 (After).
- 最好 The most good, the best: 最 (Most) + 好 (Good).

272. 意 (Yì) Meaning, intention, desire, consider.

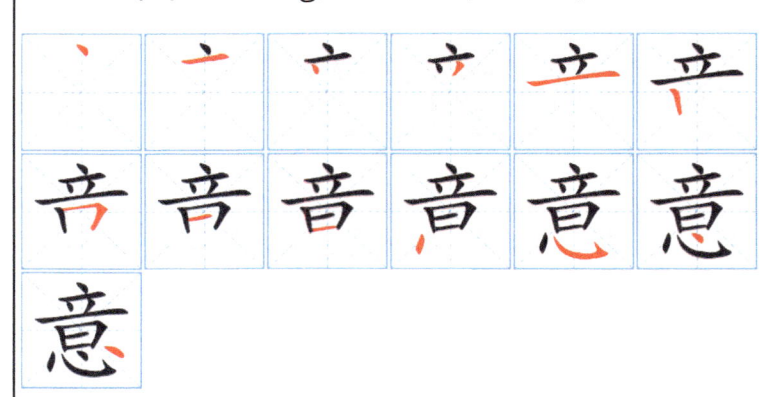

Note: Character with extended **meaning of the intentions** of the heart (心) said or expressed with sounds (音). See character no. 28 and 262.
- 意思 Meaning: 意 (Meaning) + 思 (Thinking).
- 同意 Agree: 同 (Be equal to) + 意 (Intention).
- 生意 Business: 生 (Birth) + 意 (desire).

273. 亲 (Qīn) Relative, family, marriage, intimate, dear, personally, kiss.

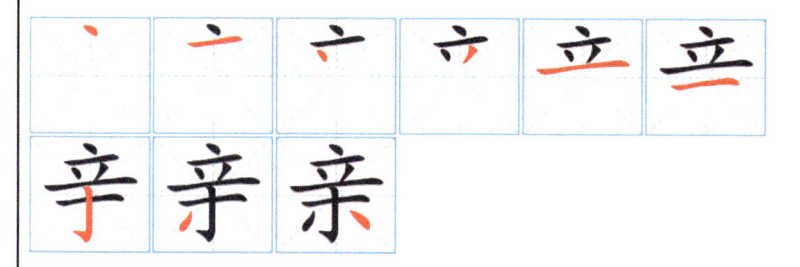

Note: Character with extended meaning of a person standing (立) very close, just an inch (寸) away, representing a family member. See character no. 64 and 166.
- 亲人 Relative: 亲 (Relative) + 人 (Person).
- 亲手 With one's own hands: 亲 (Personally) + 手 (Hand).

274. 件 (Jiàn) Article, document, item, piece, measurement word for clothing.

Note: Associative character of a person (人) with his cow (牛), his most precious **item**. See character no. 1 and 83.
- 事件 Case, incident: 事 (Thing) + 件 (Article).
- 文件 Document, file: 文 (Writing) + 件 (Document).

275. 贝 (Bèi) Shell, money.

Note: Pictogram of a shell used as **money** in ancient China.

276. 讲 (Jiǎng) Say, speak, conversation, explain, negotiate.

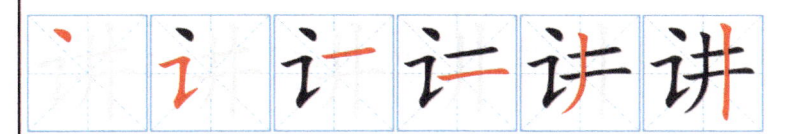

Note: Picto-phonetic character of word (言=讠) and well (井). The character on the left (言=讠) serves a semantic function, the words of a **conversation**. The character on the right, a phonetic (井 = Jǐng) reminder of its pronunciation. See character no. 133 and 243.
- 讲话 Speak, conversation: 讲 (Speak) + 话 (Word).

277. 远 (Yuǎn) Far away, distant, remote.

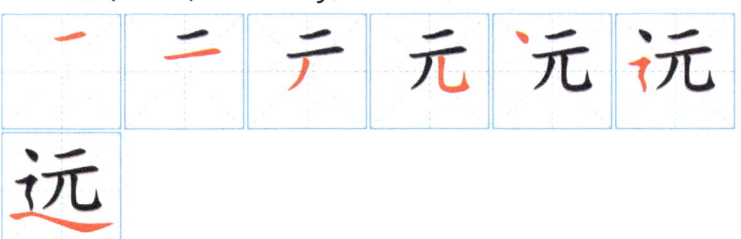

Note: Picto-phonetic character of going (走=辶) to **a distant place** looking for money (元). The character on the left (走=辶) serves a semantic function, going away. The character on the right, a phonetic (元=Yuán) reminder of its pronunciation. See character no. 61 and 123.
- 远方 Distant place: 远 (Far away) + 方 (Place).

278. 处 (Chù) Place, department, office. (Chǔ) To reside, to be situated in, to take charge of, to punish.

Note: Associative nature of a person predicting (卜) the **place** where their feet will be (足=夂) in the future. See character no. 54 and 171.
- 处理 Manage, resolve: 处 (To take charge of) + 理 (Manage).
- 文化处 Culture Office: 文 (Writing) + 化 (Change) + 处 (Place).
- 外事处 Foreign Affairs Office: 外 (Outside) + 事 (Subject) + 处 (Place).

279. 习 (Xí) Practice, exercise, learn, review, habit.

Note: Pictogram of a wing spreading to **practice** flying.
- 学习 Learn, study: 学 (Learn) + 习 (Practice).
- 自习 Learn oneself: 自 (Oneself) + 习 (Practice).

280. 寺 (Sì) Temple, monastery, palace, ancient government office.

<u>Note:</u> Associative character that represents **the place where taxes were paid** for the measures (寸) of land (土) used in agriculture. See character no. 4 and 65.

281. 运 (Yùn) Transport, carry, move, good luck.

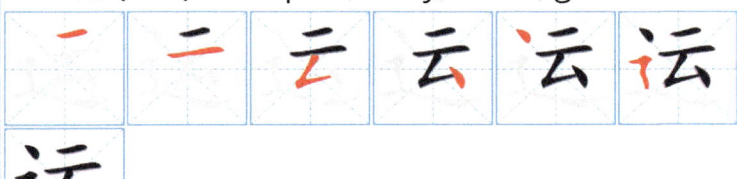

<u>Note:</u> Associative character of clouds (云) leaving (走=辶) **transporting** water. See character no. 61 and 80.
- 运动 Play sports: 运 (Move) + 动 (Move).
- 运气 Fortune, luck: 运 (Good luck) + 气 (Air).

282. 近 (Jìn) Close, get closer, get closer.

<u>Note:</u> Picto-phonetic character of walk (走=辶) and ax (斤). The character on the left (走=辶) serves a semantic function, walking and **approaching**. The character on the right, a phonetic (斤=Jīn) reminder of its pronunciation. See character no. 61 and 102.
- 最近 Recently: 最 (Most) + 近 (Get closer).
- 近亲 Close relative: 近 (Close) + 亲 (Relative).

283. 青 (Qīng) Green, blue, colors of nature, young, immature.

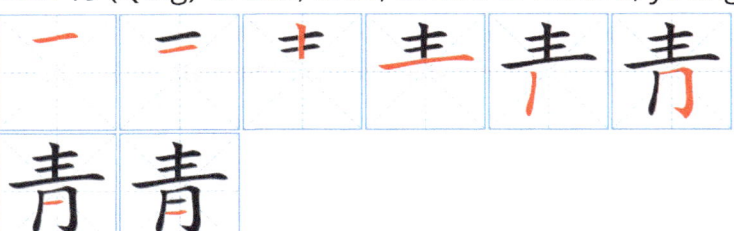

Note: Character with extended meaning of a plant being born (生) on the moon (月), representing nature and its colors. See character no. 8 and 51.
- 青天 Blue sky: 青 (Blue) + 天 (Sky).
- 青年人 Young: 青 (Young) + 年 (year) + 人 (Person).

284. 知 (Zhī) Know, realize, be aware of.

Note: Associative character of a mouth (口) responding as quickly and accurately as an arrow (矢), showing great **knowledge**. See character no. 2 and 266.
- 知道 Know: 知 (Know) + 道 (Thought).
- 认知 Knowledge: 认 (recognize) + 知 (Know).

285. 知 (Zhī) Replace, act as, generation, period of time.

Note: Associative character of a person (人) shooting an arrow with a bow (弋), thus symbolizing war and the **era changes** that it entails. See character no. 1.
- 现代 Modern times: 现 (Now) + 代 (generation).
- 代办 Act on someone's behalf: 代 (Replace) + 办 (Manage).

286. 把 (Bǎ) Grab, handle, hold, bunch, bundle.

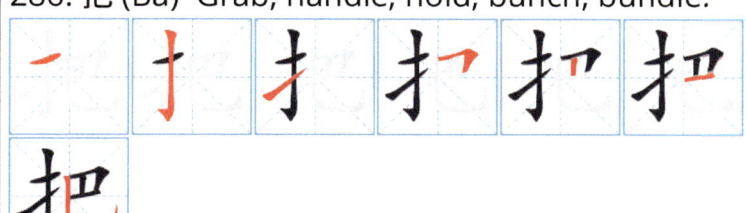

Note: Picto-phonetic character for "hand" (手 = 扌) and the character Bā (巴). The character on the left (手 = 扌) serves a semantic function, **a hand grasping something**. The character on the right, a phonetic (巴 = Bā) reminder of its pronunciation. See character no. 15 and 269.
- 一把 A handful, bunch of: 一 (One) + 把 (Bunch).
- 火把 Torch: 火 (Fire) + 把 (Hold).

287. 非 (Fēi) No, error, wrong, contrary to.

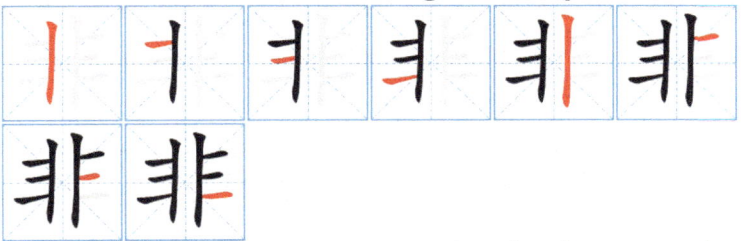

Note: Pictogram of two roads that lead to completely **opposite** destinations.
- 非法 Illegal: 非 (Contrary to) + 法 (Law).
- 是非 Good and evil: 是 (Correct) + 非 (Error).

288. 义 (Yì) Justice, righteousness, straight, just, meaning.

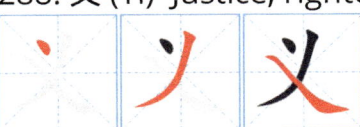

Note: Pictogram of a type of scissors used to prune and **rectify** the level of plants.
- 公义 Justice: 公 (Collective) + 义 (Justice).
- 本义 Original meaning: 本 (Base) + 义 (Meaning).
- 定义 Definition: 定 (Fix) + 义 (Meaning).

The Logic of Chinese Characters

289. 员 (Yuán) Member, person who is dedicated to some activity.

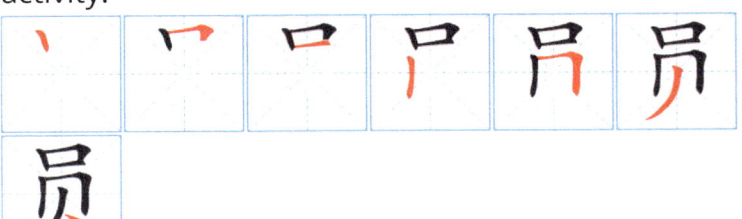

Note: Associative character of a sea shell that grants the right to speak, exemplifying **a member** of some ancient government organization.
- 员工 Employee: 员 (Member) + 工 (Work).
- 队员 Member of a team: 队 (Team) + 员 (Member).
- 打字员 Typist: 打 (Hit) + 字 (Letter) + 员 (Member).

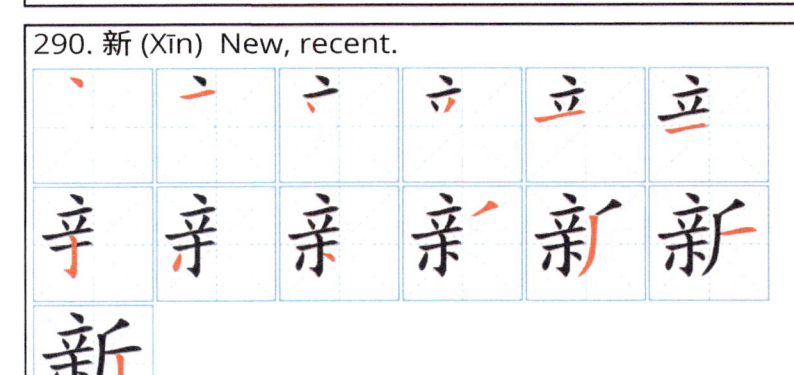

290. 新 (Xīn) New, recent.

Note: Associative character of a **new** ax (斤) brought home by a relative (亲). See character no. 102 and 173.
- 新年 New year: 新 (New) + 年 (Year).
- 新手 Beginner: 新 (New) + 手 (Hand).

291. 毛 (Máo) Hair, wool, feather.

Note: Pictogram of a lock of animal **hair**.
- 羊毛 Wool: 羊 (Sheep) + 毛 (Hair).

292. 告 (Gào) Say, announce, inform, accuse, declare.

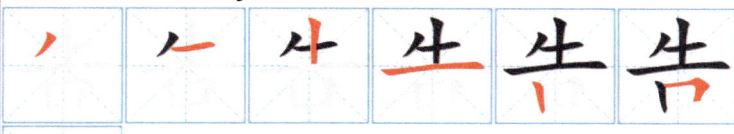

Note: Associative character of a mouth (口) informing ts god of a sacrifice of a bull (牛). See character no. 2 and 83.
- 告知 Inform: 告 (Say) + 知 (Know).
- 广告 Advertisement: 广 (Spread) + 告 (Inform).

293. 夫 (Fū) Man, husband, person who performs manual work.

Note: Pictogram of an adult man (大) with a pin in his hair (一), a sign that he had already reached the age to marry and fulfill his role as a **husband**. See character no. 5.
- 夫人 Wife, someone's lady: 夫 (Husband) + 人 (Person).

294. 情 (Qíng) Love, feeling, situation, kindness., affection, passion, sexual passion.

Note: Picto-phonetic character for heart (心=忄) and young (青). The character on the left fulfills a semantic function, the **feelings** that emanate from the heart. The character on the right, a phonetic (青=Qīng) reminder of its pronunciation. See character no. 28 and 283.
- 心情 Mood: 心 (Heart) + 情 (Situation).
- 无情 Ruthless, cruel: 无 (Not having) + 情 (Feeling).

295. 竹 (Zhú) Bamboo.

Note: Pictogram of two bamboo branches. When it is part of another character, its writing is simplified as ⺮.

296. 将 (Jiāng) Support, bring, about, through, be about to. (Jiàng) Command, general, commander.

Note: Character with extended meaning that shows a piece of meat (夕) being measured (寸) leaning on a log (丬). See character no. 65 and 206.
- 将来 In the future: 将 (Be about to) + 来 (Come).
- 将军 Army General: 将 (General) + 军 (Army).

297. 社 (Shè) Society, agency, community.

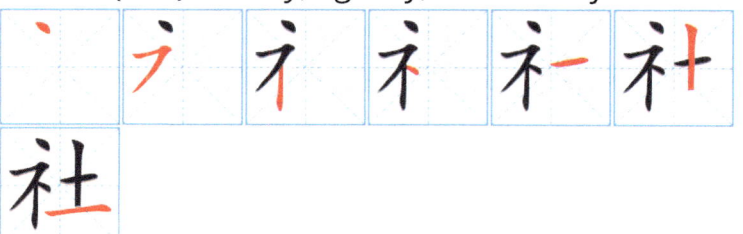

Note: Associative character of an altar (示 = 礻) used by the people of the territory (土) **society**. See character no. 4 and 265.
- 社会 Society: 社 (Society) + 会 (Society).
- 社区 Community: 社 (Community) + 区 (Zone).
- 社员 Member of a community, club, etc.: 社 (Community) + 员 (Member).

298. 父 (Fù) Father, old man.

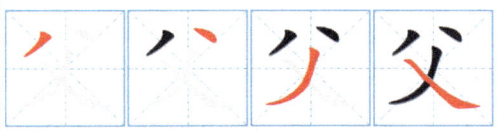

Note: Pictogram of two crossed stone axes, a symbol of the **father**'s authority.
- 父亲 Father: 父 (Father) + 亲 (Family).
- 父子 Father and son: 父 (Father) + 子 (Son).
- 天父 Heavenly Father: 天 (Sky) + 父 (Father).

299. 今 (Jīn) Today, in this moment, present.

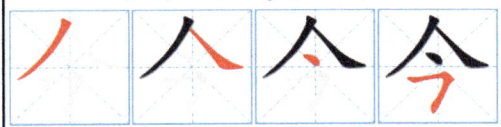

Note: Pictogram of a person standing on a cliff watching a new day, **today**. See character no. 1.
- 今天 Today: 今 (Today) + 天 (Day).
- 今年 This year: 今 (Today) + 年 (Year).

300. 语 (Yǔ) Language, proverb, saying, expression.

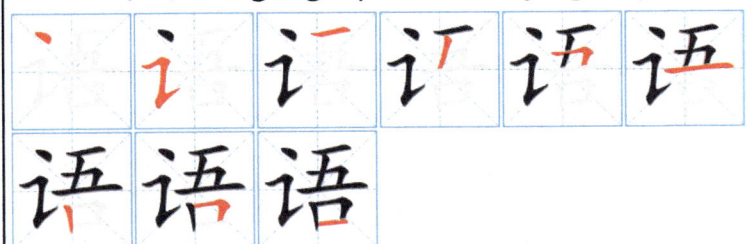

Note: Associative character of a mouth (口) speaking five (五) words (言=讠) that is, a language. See character no. 2, 133 and 249.
- 语言 Language: 语 (Language) + 言 (Word).
- 汉语 Chinese Language: 汉 (Chinese) + 语 (Language).
- 语法 Grammar: 语 (Language) + 法 (Form).

List of characters arranged alphabetically

A	Bu	Cheng	得 189	Er	G
	不 34	成 108		二 92	
An	部 254		Di	儿 60	Gan
安 127	卜 171	Chu	地 47	而 76	干 152
		出 84		尔 213	
B	C	处 278	Dian	耳 258	Gao
			电 58		高 240
Ba	Cai	D	点 221	F	告 292
八 98	才 270				
巴 269		Da	Ding	Fa	Ge
把 286	Ci	大 5	丁 164	法 129	个 42
	此 247	打 178	定 139	发 134	
Ban					Gong
办 141	Cong	Dai	Dong	Fang	工 18
	从 55	代 285	动 126	方 107	公 120
Bei			东 197		功 260
北 196	Cun	Dan		Fei	
贝 275	寸 65	但 239	Dou	飞 31	Gu
		旦 186	都 225	非 287	古 191
Ben	CH				
本 52		Dang	Dui	Fen	Guan
	Chan	当 222	兑 204	分 105	关 20
Bi	产 244		对 104		观 153
比 203		Dao	队 256	Feng	
	Chang	刀 69		风 117	Guang
Bian	长 68	道 251	Duo		广 128
边 200	厂 130	到 147	多 211	Fu	
				父 298	Guo
Bing	Che	De	E	夫 293	果 43
并 268	车 140	的 151		付 173	过 78

107

List of characters arranged alphabetically

国 67

H

Hai
还 114

Han
汉 234

Hao
好 48

He
禾 158
和 161

Hen
很 263

Hou
后 75

Hu
户 220

Hua
华 264
化 252
话 207

Hui
回 89
会 135

Huo
火 11
活 229

J

Ji
几 27
机 62
计 241

Jia
家 208
加 115

Jian
见 49
件 274
间 131

Jiang
讲 276
将 296

Jiao
叫 176

Jie
介 149

Jin
今 299
斤 102
近 282
进 253

Jing
井 243
己 109
经 226
京 182

Jiu
九 99
就 193

Jun
军 183

K

Kai
开 19

Kan
看 106

Ke
可 103

Kou
口 2

L

Lai
来 72

Lao
老 245

Le
了 30

Li
力 12
立 166
理 90
里 53

Liang
两 248

Lin
林 156

Liu

六 96

M

Ma
马 13

Mai
买 209
卖 210

Mao
毛 291

Me
么 118

Mei
美 236
没 125

Men
门 17
们 26

Mi
米 261

Mian
面 165

Mie
灭 188

Min
民 136

Ming
明 25
名 219

Mu
木 9
目 14

N

Na
那 195

Nan
男 22
南 198

Nei
内 160

Neng
能 205

Ni

108

List of characters arranged alphabetically

你 214

Nian
年 145

Niu
牛 83

Nü
女 10

O

P

Pin
品 163

Ping
平 157

Q

Qi
七 97
其 194
气 169
起 227

Qian

前 235
千 174

Qin
亲 273

Qing
情 294
青 283

Qu
去 86
区 132
取 259

Quan
全 124
犬 177

R

Ran
然 230

Rang
让 150

Ren
人 1
认 142

Ri
日 3

Rou
肉 170

Ru
如 113
入 121

S

San
三 93

Si
四 94
寺 280
思 187
丝 217

Suo
所 228

SH

Shan
山 6

Shang
上 23

Shao
勺 146
少 59

She
舌 180
社 297

Shen
什 143

Sheng
生 51

Shi
时 73
实 64
市 224
矢 266
示 265
石 155
十 100
是 57
事 231

Shou
手 15
首 237

Shu
书 267

Shui
水 7

Shuo
说 212

T

Ta
他 45
它 201
她 46

Tai
台 233
太 16

Ti
体 122

Tian
田 21
天 29

Ting
听 148

Tong
同 119

Tou
头 56

Tu
土 4

W

Wai
外 218

Wang
王 36

Wei
为 74
位 246

Wen
问 112
文 70

Wo
我 41

Wu

109

List of characters arranged alphabetically

无 249
五 95

X

Xi
夕 206
西 199
习 279

Xia
下 24

Xian
现 88

Xiang
想 111
相 79

Xiao
小 35

Xie
些 257

Xin
新 290
心 28
信 223

Xing
性 192
行 168

Xiong
兄 184

Xue
学 37

Y

Yan
言 133

Yang
羊 159
样 185

Yao
要 202

Ye
也 44
业 238

Yi
一 91
意 272
已 137

义 288
以 85

Yin
因 138
音 262

Yong
用 81

You
又 77
由 162
有 39
友 82
尤 181

Yu
玉 66
语 300
于 87
与 242

Yuan
员 289
远 277
元 123

Yue
月 170

Yun
云 80
运 281

Z

Zai
在 38

Zao
早 232

Zi
子 32
字 33
自 101

Zou
走 61

Zu
足 54

Zui
最 271

Zuo
作 215

ZH

Zhan
占 172

Zhe
着 167
者 216
这 71

Zheng
正 190
政 250

Zhi
支 255
只 110
至 144
止 179
知 284
之 116

Zhong
中 40
种 175
众 154

Zhu
主 50
竹 295

110

MORE RESOURCES TO LEARN CHINESE

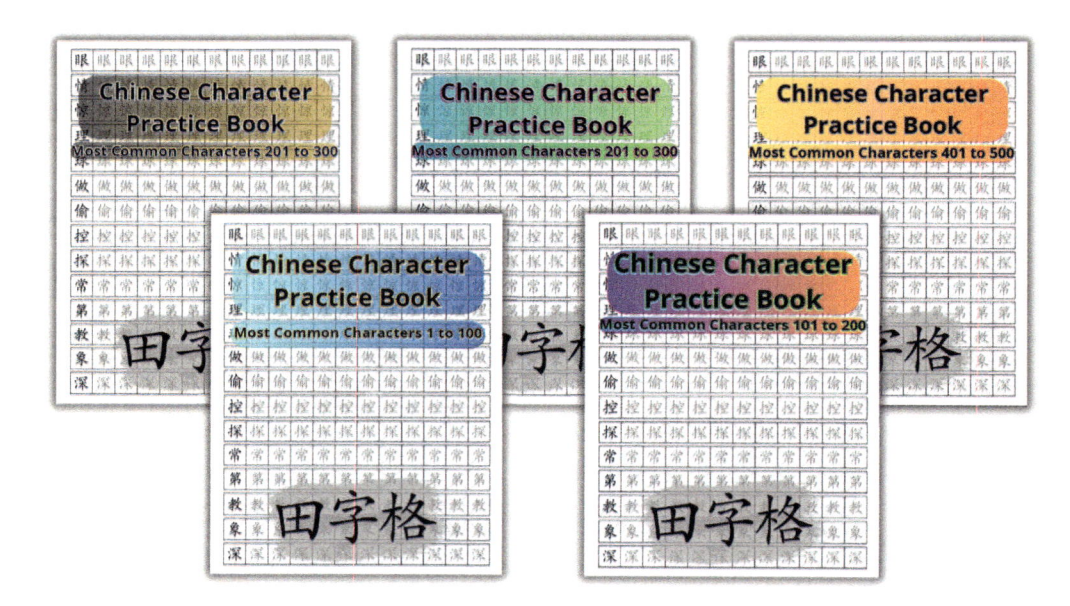

1. CHINESE CHARACTER WRITING WORKBOOK HÀNZÌ 1 TO 100   ISBN-BOCRJG2KDZ
2. CHINESE CHARACTER WRITING WORKBOOK HÀNZÌ 101 TO 200 ISBN-BOCRJ4GHCM
3. CHINESE CHARACTER WRITING WORKBOOK HÀNZÌ 201 TO 300 ISBN-BOCRJ4H7S9
4. CHINESE CHARACTER WRITING WORKBOOK HÀNZÌ 301 TO 400 ISBN-BOCRLXCC6L
5. CHINESE CHARACTER WRITING WORKBOOK HÀNZÌ 401 TO 500 ISBN-BOCRKHLCQG

MORE RESOURCES TO LEARN CHINESE

CHINESE CHARACTERS WRITING NOTEBOOK: CHINESE CHARACTERS CALLIGRAPHY NOTEBOOK
ISBN-B0CV5YCF78

LEARN CHINESE WHILE PLAYING (+100 GAMES TO LEARN CHINESE): CHILDREN'S ACTIVITIES FOR LEARNING CHINESE CHARACTERS - XXL BOOK
ISBN-B0CVRYSZDP

Printed in Great Britain
by Amazon